MW00390319

# The Kick-Ass A-Z for over 60s

## Dr Vernon Coleman

Published by EMJ Books

Vernon Coleman is a writer and the author of over 100 other books which have sold over two million hardback and paperback copies in the UK and been translated into 25 languages. Many of his books are available as Kindle books on Amazon. For a list of available eBooks please see Vernon Coleman's author page on Amazon or visit www.vernoncoleman.com (formal attire not required). Vernon Coleman is a feisty post-reconstructed pre-millennial with revolutionary tendencies.

EMJ Books, London

## Dedication

As always, to my beloved Antoinette, with all my love. No one cares more and no one is loved more.

And in memory of my parents, Kathleen and Edward Coleman, both betrayed and killed by the combined efforts of half a hundred unsympathetic and incompetent health care staff who simply didn't care enough. Too numerous to mention they all know who they are. I would like to think they learnt something. But I fear that might be too much to hope for.

## Introduction

Replace the knowing, depressing, pessimistic certainties of crabbed old age with a wild, unfettered imagination and with the hope and confidence-drenched ambition usually thought to be associated exclusively with the young.

Retain your freedom, dignity, independence and sense of humour. Stay young in spirit, start again at 65 and live another life for free.

Never let the bastards grind you down. (They will try. Believe me, they will try.)

And remember: if you are over 65, your government wants you dead. So screw 'em. Live a long, happy and boisterous second life. You owe it to yourself.

This is the beginners' guide to older age; an A to Z handbook for the funny side of life.

*Vernon Coleman*

# A

## ABUSE

How unbelievably awful it is that doctors and nurses accept that the elderly (historically the over 65s, now the over 60s and soon to be the over 50s) must be allowed to die because keeping them alive isn't cost effective. The official attitude is that old people don't matter and don't have rights simply because they are old.

Some time ago, a Select Committee on Human Rights, comprised of MPs and peers, reported that 21% of British hospitals and care homes failed to meet even minimum standards of dignity and privacy for older people.

The Committee said it had uncovered evidence of neglect, abuse, discrimination and unfair treatment of frail, older people. Their discovery came as no surprise to those of us who have been uncovering such abuse for decades.

Nothing was done to correct their findings.

And it is generally agreed that since then things have deteriorated considerably.

## ACTIVE

Try to remain as active as you can for as long as you can. Most people can still get around, even if they are frail and would find running a mile a bit of a challenge. Give yourself more time if you need to walk somewhere or go up a long flight of stairs. Take a rest every now and then. If anyone complains, hit them with a stick. (I recommend carrying a large stick even if you don't need it for support. Sticks are very useful for hitting, prodding and poking people who have annoyed or patronised you. They are also useful for fending off over-friendly dogs who look hungry). Don't be suckered into buying a mobility scooter. Too many people use mobility scooters when they don't really need them. Leave mobility scooters for fat and lazy 29-year-olds who are doomed anyway.

Staying physically active can help you financially. Instead of hiring a gardener to mow your lawn, do it yourself for as long as you can. Instead of paying a bunch of Romanians to wash your car, buy a sponge and a hose and do it yourself.

# AGEISM

We live in a politically correct world but the elderly don't count – particularly if they are white and English. Elderly patients in hospital are ignored by staff and left to starve to death, denied even water if they cannot get out of bed and fetch it themselves. It is common for elderly patients to be left in pain, lying in soiled bed clothes.

Old people are a burden which the governments have decided they cannot afford, and so the politicians will continue to authorise whatever methods are necessary to ensure that the number of burdensome old people is kept to a minimum.

In February 2011, an official UK report condemned the NHS for its 'inhumane treatment of elderly patients' and stated that NHS hospitals were 'failing to meet even the most basic standards of care' for the over-65s. Nothing was done to correct this.

It is no exaggeration to say that the NHS still treats the elderly with complete contempt. If animals were treated the same way there would, quite rightly, be an outcry. (It used to be said that you can judge a civilisation by the way it treats its elderly.)

The problem is that if you are over 65-years-old your government wants you dead. And so it is now official Government policy to ignore the needs of the elderly. Doctors and nurses are told to let old people die – and to withhold treatment which might save their lives. When doctors and nurses are employed by, and therefore owned by, the Government then the Government's priorities take over. And so the elderly, who are regarded as an expensive burden, are considered expendable. Hospital staff are told to deprive the elderly of food and water so that they die rather than take up valuable hospital beds. The only -ism that no one cares about is ageism.

The startling, sad truth is that ageism is today the acceptable face of prejudice, bigotry and discrimination. People who would not dream of expressing prejudice towards people of another colour or race will quite happily express outrageously prejudiced views about the elderly. Individuals who regard themselves as entirely free of bigotry will merrily express bigoted remarks about the elderly. And the desperately and determinedly politically correct who proudly consider themselves entirely free of any tendency towards discrimination will, apparently without regret, discriminate against the elderly without a second thought; apparently without any thought that they might be behaving badly.

Just a few generations ago, it was widely believed that citizens who had black skin were not entitled to be treated as fully paid up members of the human race. Within living memory, women were not allowed to vote because they were considered inferior to men. And it is only within the last few decades that homosexuality has become accepted behaviour.

Most people in our society now like to proclaim themselves to be 'liberal' in their attitude towards their fellow men and women. Anyone who uses any old-fashioned phrase now considered unacceptable by the 'thought-police' is likely to find themselves crushed by opprobrium. Anyone who makes a modestly patronising remark about women, homosexuals or members of any religious group is likely to find him or herself standing in the dock, grovelling, expressing remorse and apologising endlessly.

But it is, it seems, perfectly acceptable to abuse and mistreat anyone over the age of a certain age without recourse.

It still staggers me that in the United Kingdom it has, for some years, been perfectly legal for doctors and nurses to murder anyone who can be described as 'elderly' and therefore regarded as an expensive and troublesome burden. And I find it difficult to believe (but it is a fact) that staff working in nursing homes are allowed to medicate the elderly against their will and without their knowledge; doping them with tranquillisers and sedatives in order to make them less troublesome to care for.

The truth is that individuals who sneer at the elderly are the same people who used to sneer at blacks, women, invalids and Jews. They are, to put it simply, prejudiced bigots.

There is a good deal that is wrong with health care these days.

We live in a world where it is considered acceptable for men and women to have to share a ward; where hospital bathrooms are so dirty that patients dare not use them; where dentists are so scarce and expensive that people have to resort to pulling their own bad teeth with the aid of a length of string tied to a doorknob.

But it is the elderly who, above all others, are regarded as disposable and irrelevant. It is the elderly who have no rights. Sexism and racism are outlawed but ageism is not. Indeed, ageism is now a State sponsored prejudice.

Violent, feral youths who are caught assaulting elderly law-abiding citizens are likely to be 'punished' with a fistful of vouchers entitling them to a handful of free CDs (the lyrics of which may well encourage more violence) but honest, elderly citizens who, cannot afford to pay their council tax bill will end up in prison.

Traditionally the elderly were consulted and regarded as repositories of wisdom, knowledge and experience. Not now. Today, the elderly are assumed to be slow-witted, out of touch and stupid. They are thrown on the scrapheap and patronised by 25-year-old 'know it alls' who spend their days reinventing the wheel and rediscovering stuff we knew decades ago. This is inevitable because they are young and ignorant, they have read little and they have experienced less. Worse still, they are too arrogant to ask or listen or even acknowledge that they might not know everything. We have to live in a world run by hubristic individuals with the emotional and intellectual age of 14-year-olds.

The age at which citizens are officially regarded as nothing more than a cumbersome nuisance has been falling steadily for years.

Today, anyone over the age of 65 is likely to be regarded as worthless. It has been repeatedly suggested that those over 65 should not be allowed to vote and that euthanasia for the over 65s should be made widely available (and involuntary). But those ages are falling rapidly.

The truth is that the commonest and most limiting factors affecting the elderly are not ill-health or disability but social and imaginary, a result of myth and prejudice and a deliberate, cold-blooded lack of care or caring.

Today, old age often leads to poverty, a lack of dignity and brutal indifference from vast swathes of society.

The elderly, above all others, live in a culture of neglect.

The current generation of oldies built their nation's prosperity by hard work but they are now demeaned, harried, pushed around and, to a large extent, politically disenfranchised.

Being rude or patronising about oldsters is acceptable in the way that being rude about blacks, women, gays, etc., would not be allowed.

Younger people oppress the aged without seeming to realise that they themselves are one day going to join that oppressed minority.

The elderly who have physical weaknesses are ignored and isolated in a way we would never dream of ignoring or isolating a 30-year-old with the same problem. Surveys and television ratings stop at the age of 50. No one cares about the elderly or what they think or feel or want.

But most of all ageism is endemic in health care.

A reader wrote to tell me that when she visited her doctor complaining of painful knees her doctor told her, very abruptly, that her problem was that she was living too long. She was devastated. 'It wasn't said as a joke,' she told me. 'He meant it.'

In the months before he died, my father repeatedly complained: 'People treat me like a fool because I am old'.

A 79-year-old reader told me: 'If you are over 55 they want you dead because you're too expensive alive.'

So, the bottom line is: stick up for yourself.

Remember the old man who went to see a doctor complaining of a pain in his left shoulder.

'What do you expect, at your age?' demanded the doctor gruffly.

'My other shoulder is the same age, and that doesn't hurt,' replied the old man.


## ATTITUDE

Around 75% of old age is down to attitude. You're still the person that you were half a century ago. You've just been around for longer. Remember that most old people don't feel any different inside.

# AMBITION

Have five and ten year goals and ambitions.

Purpose will prolong your life more than anything. Ambitions will focus your attention and make your life more worthwhile.

Make a list of things you would like to do, want to do, intend to do and want to have done within your five and ten year time scales.

Don't be satisfied with a dull bucket list of places you want to visit and silly things you want to do. Bigger ambitions will be far more satisfying.

Most people who have had great ideas had them early in life. This is not because young people are brainier than old people (they aren't) but because when we are new to a subject we are less hampered by preconceived ideas. It is a lot easier to look at something with a fresh and creative eye when you have only been studying it for a relatively short period.

So, if you start to study new areas you will be more likely to come up with original thoughts.

If people changed jobs every decade or so they would get more out of life (and put far more into it) than they do. If cardiologists retrained as barristers or film directors or even as geriatricians they would be far more likely to have great new ideas.

For most of us this is impractical. But for the elderly it is an extremely practical notion.

Plan ahead. At 70, you can enjoy freedom and adventure you only dreamt of at 17 or 27 when your life was constrained by fears and the dread of embarrassment.

You had one life: now start again with the benefit of hindsight to enrich your expectations.

Life is too valuable to spend it surfing the bloody internet, reading a newspaper all the way through or watching daytime television.

If nothing else, remember that your government wants you dead. That should be incentive enough to hang around for as long as possible.

# B

## BASTARDS

Never let the bastards grind you down. The world contains far more than its fair share of bastards and the older you get the more you will realise that too often it is the bastards who make the rules and answer the telephone. If they are rude and aggressive to you, feel free to be rude and aggressive to them. If they complain and things get nasty, you can always use the 'I'm old and a bit dotty' as a get out of jail free card.

## BED REST

Bed rest is a killer. It is no accident that loads of people die in bed. All sorts of terrible things happen if you stay in bed too long – especially if you're over the age of 60. Blood clots form in the veins, muscles waste, bones decalcify, lungs fill with fluid and the brain rapidly rots. Official statistics show clearly that far more people die in bed than die lying down in the middle of the road. Bed is a dangerous place.

## BED SORES

The incidence of bed sores is increasing rapidly. There are exceptions but generally speaking, bed sores are a sign of incompetent nursing. In the bad old days, when hospitals were run by matrons and ward sisters, it was a sign of shame to find a patient with a bedsore. And that was before the introduction of ripple beds. These days, bed sores are endemic in many hospitals and institutions because nurses are too busy attending meetings to check their patients or turn them. If a patient develops a bed sore then it is generally speaking because the quality of nursing provided has been somewhere between poor and appalling. It is much easier to prevent a small bed sore from developing into a big one than it is to cure a big one.

## BEETHOVEN

'Take life by the throat', said Beethoven who took his own advice and won his personal battle with life and deafness by a technical knock-out. (Then, when he was safely dead, the EU bastards nicked one of his best tunes as an anthem.)

## BEREAVEMENT

You should not feel bad if you suffer enormously when you are bereaved. The fact is that bereavement for the old is just as painful as it is for the young. Ignore the soulless, crass morons who say things such as 'He had a good innings' or 'Well she had a good, long life' in the apparent belief that such drivel makes everything all right.

It has always confused me that people dismiss as merely inevitable, of very little consequence and almost irrelevant, when an old person dies.

The older person who has died almost certainly knew that he or she was dying and almost certainly didn't want to die.

And the old person who dies is likely to have a spouse, a family, friends and neighbours who are likely to be devastated. They will have lost someone whom they have known for decades or more. And yet they will probably have to deal with their loss with very little support.

It is perfectly sensible, logical and proper for anyone who loses an elderly relative or friend to be devastated.

If you are close to someone who is elderly and frail, you should plan for bereavement.

You should be prepared for whatever economic and practical problems that will lie ahead. Most people who are bereaved find that they have to get through at least two months of confusion. They will be vulnerable, both physically and mentally, for at least a year.

Everyone (whatever their age) should make some plans for bereavement. It helps, for example, if basic bills (heating and so on) are paid by direct debit so that they do not get forgotten.

## BLOODY MINDEDNESS

Bloody mindedness may not be a popular quality and it may not win you friends among life's prefects but it is, generally speaking, more of a virtue rather than a curse. 'Do not go gently into that good night' wrote Dylan Thomas in a remarkable moment of comparative sobriety.

The fact is that the bloody-minded live longer – especially if they are marooned in one of those appalling places we call hospitals, where the general aim of the staff is to send everyone over the age of 60 down to the morgue as quickly as possible.

You should complain a good deal and ask as many questions as you can think of; you should make a fuss and remind everyone in a uniform or a white coat that you are a human being; you should be forever aware of your dignity and your self-respect.

Sticking up for yourself might not make you popular but you aren't in hospital to make friends. Influencing people to regard you with more respect will mean that you will be treated better and you will, as a result, be more likely to survive the miserable experience.

## BREAST CANCER

Breast cancer is one of the most constantly publicised and most greatly feared forms of cancer. Because of its very nature, it is a type of cancer which arouses much emotion. Newspapers, magazines and medical journals have for decades been full of articles describing new forms of treatment and the cancer charities, not known for their honesty or modesty, are forever boasting of new cures. Lies are spread, myths are created. Sadly, these boasts are generally invented in order to gain more funds and most are quickly forgotten. The medical journal, *The Lancet*, in an editorial, commented that: 'If one were to believe all the media hype, the triumphalism of the profession in published research, and the almost weekly miracle breakthroughs trumpeted by the cancer charities, one might be surprised that women are dying at all from this cancer.'

Only fairly recently was it finally admitted that the incidence of breast cancer was rising and that many cases of breast cancer are caused by diet.

For three decades I have been pointing out that breast cancer (probably above all others) is linked directly to diet and, in particular, to the consumption of cheap, fatty meat.

My attempts to publicise this proven truth were made infinitely more difficult by organisations such as the Advertising Standards Authority (which banned advertisements for my book *Food for Thought* because it truthfully linked cancer to meat consumption) and the Press Complaints Commission (which rolled over obediently when asked to do so by the meat trade and condemned me for daring to publicise the truth about the meat-cancer link).

Since 1942, there has been steadily accumulating evidence to show that there is a link between breast cancer and dietary fat. Breast cancer could have been turned into a relatively uncommon disease, instead of one of the major killers of women, if politicians and doctors had been prepared to take on the food industry – and force the cancer industry to spread the truth.

But how many doctors now advocate a low fat, meat free diet for women who are regarded as susceptible to breast cancer? Very few – if any. Most prefer to prescribe drugs or to recommend the surgical removal of healthy breasts.

Where, sadly, is the financial profit opportunity in merely recommending a dietary change?

There has been much talk of a breast cancer gene (BRCA-1) but there isn't really any such thing. There is no gene which *causes* breast cancer. There is, however, a gene which increases a woman's chances of developing cancer. And women with this gene can dramatically reduce their risk of developing breast cancer by avoiding the factors which are known to be associated with breast cancer. They should, for example, avoid becoming overweight, cut out meat completely and eat a low fat diet. Women who are overweight have more fat in their bodies and are more likely to develop cancer of the breast. The modern 'scientific' approach (to remove the healthy breasts of women who have the breast cancer gene) is barbaric and unnecessary.

In my book *2020* (which was published in 2010) I forecast that the incidence of breast cancer in China would rise. It was not a difficult prediction. The Chinese people, growing in wealth, are dramatically increasing their intake of meat. When the same thing happened in Japan a few years ago, the result was a dramatic increase in the incidence of breast cancer in Japanese women. The ones who stuck to a low-meat traditional Japanese diet were far less likely to develop breast cancer when compared to the women who changed to a high-meat American style diet. Just a little more than a year after I wrote *2020* it was revealed that my prediction was already coming true.

The main problem is that the meat sold today causes far more cancer than ever before because it is fattier than ever and the fat is full of carcinogens.

There are two reasons for this.

First, farmers who sell heavy, fatty animals get more money than they would get for thinner, lighter animals.

Second, farmers use carcinogenic chemicals on their farms. And those chemicals end up in the animal's fat.

It is these two facts which explain why the incidence of cancer always rises when populations start eating more meat.

But why is the incidence of breast cancer particularly likely to rise?

The answer to that is simple too.

When animals eat toxic substances such as carcinogenic chemicals which have been sprayed on the grass or put into the food they eat, the deadly chemicals are stored in the animals' fatty tissues.

The fattier the animal is, the more carcinogens it will have stored in its body. And, when it is killed and eaten, those carcinogens will be consumed by the person eating the meat. And, as with animals, the carcinogens will tend to gravitate to, and be stored in, the fatty tissues.

And the human breasts contain a good deal of fat.

Indeed, there is remarkably little actual breast tissue in a breast. Most of the breast is fat. And the bigger the breast the more fat there is likely to be. This is why breast cancer is commoner among older women. They tend to have more fat on their bodies in general and to have bigger and fattier breasts in particular. Poorer people tend to eat fattier meat. That's why poor people tend to get more cancer than rich people.

But sadly, as I've already said, instead of discouraging women from eating meat, doctors prefer to remove healthy breasts from women considered genetically susceptible to breast cancer.

Utter bloody madness!


# CANCER

Cancer is, along with heart disease, stroke and doctors, one of the four big killers of our time.

But cancer is undoubtedly the killer that frightens people most. The very word is so emotive that most doctors try not to use it when talking to patients. Instead of talking of cancer they talk of 'tumours' and 'growths'. They know that cancer is something most people don't even like to talk about so they don't talk about it either.

In order to ensure that money continues to pour in, the cancer industry must persuade potential contributors and supporters that it is making progress in the fight against cancer. And so there are frequent news releases about exciting new cancer remedies. Some of these widely promoted new treatments are in the early stages of being tested on human patients, some have not yet being tested on humans but are promoted as the new 'wonder' cure for cancer on the basis of preliminary and entirely unreliable animal experiments, and some are talked about as new 'breakthroughs' largely or even exclusively on the basis of a scientist's theory or hypothesis.

These news stories raise hopes falsely and distract attention and finance from those areas which really need it (the prevention of cancer and the care of those who have cancer) but they serve the purpose: they raise money for the cash-hungry cancer industry.

Generally speaking, the cancer industry is a failure. Mortality figures show that more people are dying from commoner forms of cancer now than they were a generation ago. One in three people already has, or will develop, cancer.

The fact that the incidence of cancer has increased dramatically during the 20th and 21st centuries confirms the view that cancer is, to a large extent, a man-made disease, created largely by our changing diet and our addiction to tobacco and meat as well as our exposure to chemicals and pollution. Researchers found only one case of cancer among hundreds of Egyptian mummies and by the 19th century, cancer was still a relatively uncommon disease. According to Garrison's *History of Medicine* the disease only began to show an 'alarming increase' in the early part of the 20th century.

It is strange, is it not, that so many campaigners spend much public money on promoting the dubious notion that man-made climate change is threatening our planet's existence but spend nothing at all on sharing the provable truth that cancer is, very largely, a man-made disease and its influence can, therefore, be limited.

Scientists who have assessed the value of the war against cancer agree that we are losing the fight and that there is no evidence to suggest that decades of expensive research have had much, if any, effect on the most fundamental measure of success or failure – death.

In areas where cancer has become more amenable to treatment, or now takes fewer lives, it is usually changes in lifestyle which are responsible – not discoveries made in the laboratory.

There are, I believe, several reasons why those fighting the war against cancer are losing.

In my book *Paper Doctors* (published in 1977) I complained that: 'Medical researchers involved in publicly or charitably financed cancer research, persist in looking for the 'magical cure'.

Much laboratory work has been started on the mistaken assumption that there is one disease called 'cancer' and that there will be a 'cure' which will enable doctors to treat all the patients suffering with cancer. Many projects have been funded because organisers (both qualified and lay) believed that they might solve the problem of cancer once and for all to the well-publicised credit of everyone concerned. The cancer industry still spends a vast fortune every year searching for the silver bullet. According to one honest observer: 'Basic cancer research is an excellent slush fund for molecular biologists but it won't have any impact on cancer'.

The bottom line is that cancer is created by chemical pollutants, by unhealthy, fatty, food and by tobacco. Poisoned water supplies, dangerous prescription drugs and the overuse of X-rays have also contributed to the incidence of cancer.

With immune systems constantly battered by polluted air, adulterated and chemically impregnated food, and a constant onslaught from the drugs we buy for ourselves, or allow our doctors to prescribe for us, it is not surprising that increasing numbers of people succumb to one of the many different types of cancer.

It is astonishing but true that we know what causes 80% of all cases of cancer. Eight out of ten people who develop cancer could have been saved if money and effort had been put into prevention. If I had the annual income the cancer industry enjoys, I believe that I could turn cancer into a historical oddity within five years.

Sadly, however, the cancer research industry is exactly that – an industry. It is a massive, worldwide multi-billion dollar industry which employs hundreds of thousands of scientists and administrators. If the cancer industry spent its income on explaining to people how to avoid cancer, there would be little or no place for research laboratories and a great many scientists would be put out of work. Worse still, if the cancer industry reduced the number of people dying of cancer, its own income would fall. This may sound cynical but it is the truth.

And so it is the scientists searching for laboratory cures who get the big grants and the prestigious awards and who are fussed over and praised by the politicians and the journalists.

Consumers quite like the idea of someone finding a 'cure' for cancer because it means that they can carry on eating the fatty food they like and smoking the cigarettes they enjoy without having to worry.

Looking for a magical cure for cancer has been an expensive and unrewarding exercise.

Cancer treatment hasn't been much, if any, better.

General speaking, the treatment methods of choice (surgery, chemotherapy and radiation therapy) have not improved mortality rates. There have been some very important advances in cancer treatment in recent years. But they have been largely limited to rare cancers that tend to occur in children and young adults, and those make up only perhaps one or two per cent of the total cancer burden. There has been little or no improvement in the death rates for the big killers: lung cancer, breast cancer, prostate cancer or cancer of the colon.

Governments have failed to teach their citizens the facts about cancer for two reasons.

First, governments are always wary of annoying big, powerful, tax-paying industries and there is absolutely no doubt that many huge, international corporations would be (to put it mildly) exceedingly upset if millions of potential consumers were, for example, warned of the dangers of eating meat.

Second, governments do not want people to live longer. On the contrary, they have a vested interest in people not living too long. People who live on into their 60s, 70s and 80s have to be given pensions and cost Governments a great deal of money.

Remember that we know what causes 80% of all cancers. If people ate less fatty food and avoided meat, the incidence of cancer would plummet.

And it is never too late to adjust your diet. The American National Academy of Sciences, has concluded that 'cancers of most major sites are influenced by dietary factors'. It has been estimated that 'a little more than 40% of cancers in men and almost 60% of cancers in women in the United States could be attributed to dietary factors'.

It is almost certainly the chemicals in fatty meat which cause cancer and there is no little irony in the fact that the pharmaceutical industry makes billions of dollars selling drugs for the treatment of cancers which some believe may have been created by its billion dollar sister industry: the chemical industry.

So, now you know.

Whether you do anything with the knowledge you have is entirely up to you.


# CARE HOMES

The term 'care home' is a misnomer and is widely used to describe residential establishments where elderly folk are supposed to be 'cared for' but are too often regarded as cash cows and nuisances.

In the United Kingdom, one quarter of all care homes have been officially classified as unsafe and the real figure is undoubtedly much higher. This scary information is of no value, however, since the Government refuses to publish a list of the worst care homes.

My advice is that you should avoid all residential establishments which specialise in looking after the elderly. If you simply need to go somewhere safe and warm where you will be looked after, treated politely, provided with regular meals and able to sleep in clean sheets then I recommend that you move into a hotel. You will probably find the bills considerably lower, particularly if you negotiate a long-term rate, and you will be far less likely to catch one of the lethal infections which infest all hospitals and quasi hospital institutions. In a hotel, you won't be given tea which has sleeping tablets dissolved in it, you will meet a wider variety of people and you may even have access to a swimming pool and a games room. In general hotels are better, cheaper and far more fun. No hotel would survive for long if it provided the sort of appalling food served up in health care institutions. And similarly no hotel would survive if the staff treated their residents in the same offhand way that most care home staff treat their patients.

## CATARACT

Cataracts occur commonly in older eyes. Here's a trick most doctors won't bother to tell you: if you have a cataract you will be able to read more easily if you have a specific light directed onto the book you are reading, and turn off the room lights. Samuel Pepys knew this but most doctors don't.

## CELEBRITIES

Celebrity luvvies need publicity the same as the rest of us need oxygen and food.

In order to satisfy their craving, and feed their inestimably large egos, they need to pontificate (via Twitter and Facebook) at least six times a day. You cannot be a celebrity these days unless you have a Twitter account and a few million twats (as I believe they are called) following your every thought.

Sadly, however, I don't remember ever hearing the celebrity types who have appointed themselves as self-appointed saviours of mankind, talking much about old people.

The celebrity lefty luvvies who like to share their sympathy for Syrian refugees and asylum seeking terrorists know that they won't get quoted in the papers if they tweet about vanilla white old people freezing to death or struggling to live on one tin of beans a week.

Britain is rich enough to spend over £100 billion on a new rail link (widely regarded as unnecessary) between London and somewhere a bit further north. And we have for years apparently considered ourselves rich enough to waste billions every year on foreign aid (most of it is creamed off by greedy consultants and self-serving charities).

Oh, and, apparently, rich enough to pay £350 million a week for membership of the European Union.

And yet between 60,000 and 100,000 elderly citizens die of cold every winter in the United Kingdom.

How can we possibly call ourselves civilised when so many elderly citizens can't afford to keep warm in cold weather?

If 60,000 asylum seekers died of the cold, the liberal lefty luvvies would be twittering as fast as their fingers could fly. They would be appalled. They would demand action.

But they don't give a toss about elderly Britons.

The elderly are our oppressed and forgotten people.

More than a million old people who have trouble surviving receive no help whatsoever. Nothing.

Moreover, a contact working in an English hospital tells me that elderly patients are deliberately put onto wards where the killer infection caused by the MRSA bug is endemic in order to get rid of them as quickly as possible.

(Could this be one of the reasons hospitals seem apparently reluctant to take the simple steps that would eradicate killer, antibiotic resistant bugs?)

In every conceivable way, the elderly are poorer today than ever before.

And yet our politicians don't give a stuff. As far as they are concerned, the elderly are merely a nuisance. And an expensive nuisance at that. (Worse still, they tend to be patriotic, remember Hitler and want to leave the EU.)

And the Entitlement Generation are too busy thinking of themselves to give a toss about the elderly.

What the politicians and the Entitlement Generation forget is that one day they too will be old.

By then they will have helped build a society in which anyone over the age of 60 is regarded as worthless and disposable.


## CENTARIANS

When several hundred American centarians were questioned about their health, a pleasing 17% said their health was excellent, a delightful 39% said it was good, a modest 33% said their health could only be described as fair and only 9% said their health was poor or very poor.

Live a healthy enough life to get to 100 and you will probably stay reasonably healthy.


## CHARITIES

Most charities are bad organisations and, despite their claims and their advertisements, they are not your friend. Not a few organisations which claim to care for the elderly have been exposed as taking advantage of older citizens. Most such charities have very high paid salaries and a good proportion of the money they raise is spent on huge salaries, fat pensions and generous pension accounts. I wouldn't trust any large, national charity to help me across the road.

Charities are big business these days and even the well-known, apparently respectable ones, are intolerably aggressive, greedy, demanding. Most charities spend most of their money on salaries and marketing – with surprisingly little of the loot going to the intended source.

Worse still, charities relentlessly harass the elderly because they know they tend to be kinder and more susceptible to a sob story than others. And the minute you give money to one charity you will become a target. They will mail you time and time again. They will harass you on the telephone and by email. They will send people round to knock on your door. And they will sell your name and details to other grasping charities too.

My advice is that you should never, ever give your address or bank account details or credit card details to a so-called charity worker – especially one who stops you in the street. Most of these are chuggers, hired on behalf of large charities to solicit contributions. They have no interest in the charity concerned and a good chunk of your money will go to the company which employs them. You will be better served, and you will serve your community more effectively, by giving whatever you want to give to small, specific local charities which are run by honest, committed and genuinely well-meaning volunteers and which have a clear, specific purpose.

And, remember, don't trust a charity to provide you with honest advice on any issue.

Other organisations which claim to provide services for the elderly are businesses which have made millions by targeting the vulnerable.

So, for example, I used to have house insurance with a company specialising in providing cover for the elderly until I discovered I could buy exactly the same cover elsewhere at a quarter of the cost.

# CHECK UPS

Most health check-ups are a waste of energy and time and more likely to do harm. (See Screening below.) The two exceptions are eye tests and dental check-ups. Eye tests are useful because a properly done test should include a test for glaucoma (a condition which can cause blindness if left untreated). Dental checks are useful partly because rotting teeth and ill-fitting dentures can make life painful and miserable but also because tooth infections are a possible cause of deadly sepsis.

Don't bother paying for a medical check-up.

And those check-ups offered by a GP are usually likely to do more harm than good. It is a good idea to have your blood pressure checked every six months or so but you don't need a doctor or a nurse to do that. You can buy an effective sphygmomanometer (blood pressure testing machine) quite cheaply. Check your blood pressure every three months or so. If it seems high then sit quietly and then take it again a couple of minutes later. Do this three times. If the reading is still high then visit your doctor and ask him to take it.

It is also a good idea to get to know your own body and to learn to spot any changes or abnormalities.

You should see a doctor without delay if:

You have any unexplained bleeding – from anywhere.

You have any unexplained pain which recurs or which lasts more than five days. (Obviously, severe pain needs to be investigated without delay.)

You need to take any self-prescribed medicine for five days or more.

You notice any persistent change in your body (e.g. a loss or gain in weight, a paralysis of any kind or the development of any lump or swelling).

Any existing skin lump, wart or blemish of any kind changes size or colour or bleeds.

You notice new symptoms when you have received medical treatment.

There are mental symptoms present, such as confusion, amnesia, paranoia, disorientation or severe depression

# CHOLESTEROL

There are over nearly ten million people in Britain now taking cholesterol-lowering 'superdrugs'. In July 2008, it was revealed that these drugs might cause problems. Readers of my book *How To Stop Your Doctor Killing You* have been aware of the problems associated with these drugs since 1996. Despite the dangers, the cholesterol lowering drugs are widely advertised and promoted – even though I don't believe there is evidence that these drugs are safe or useful enough for such mass consumption.

In January 2011, it was reported that seven million people in the UK were taking drugs called statins, theoretically to prevent heart attacks. Encouraged by the drug industry, GPs were, at a huge cost to the NHS, prescribing the damned things for everyone with a pulse.

The big joke is that no one really knows whether reducing cholesterol levels does more harm than good.

The big drug companies that make all this junk are, of course, laughing all the way to the bank.


# CONFIDENTIALITY

Medical confidentiality is now a historical concept. The medical profession has abandoned all pretence at offering patients anything remotely resembling confidentiality. Everything you tell your doctor will be regarded as suitable to be disseminated publicly. I am not exaggerating. For many years, I fought for the principle of medical confidentiality. I lost. The General Medical Council has destroyed the principle of confidentiality.


# COVERT MEDICATION

It is now common practice in care homes, nursing homes and hospitals for staff to use nasty little tricks in order to persuade their patients to take tranquillisers and sedatives. This is, of course, not done for the sake of the patients but for the sake of the staff. Patients who lie in bed all day, doing nothing, saying nothing and asking for nothing are much easier to look after than patients who are alert and alive to the fact that they are treated by a bunch of psychopaths masquerading as nursing staff. Medicines are routinely hidden in food or drink so that residents do not know that they are being drugged. And relatives will not be made privy to the secret. Covert medication is common and, surprisingly, it is entirely legal.

As a general rule, if you go into any sort of residential home or hospital and find the majority of the residents sitting in chairs or lying in bed, silent and unspeaking, then the chances are high that everyone has been covertly medicated so that the staff can spend their days playing cards, watching television, reading the newspaper, gossiping or, on fine days, sitting out in the garden catching a few rays.

## CROOKS

There have always been crooks around who will take advantage of the innocence, naivety and gentle nature of the elderly. The advent of the internet has made it easy for financial tricksters to steal your money by emptying your online bank account. Banks have made life very easy for thieves.

Never answer questions about your money on the phone or on the internet.

The smiling rogues who ring your doorbell and tell you that your roof needs repairing or your drive needs relaying are crooks. No honest workman does this.

People who knock on your doctor and offer to appraise your antiques are really there because they want to steal your purse – or buy your valuables at a rock bottom price.

Even residential homes are packed with crooks who know all sorts of clever ways to part you from your belongings.

In many such long-stay homes, it is common for a member of staff to remove all rings and other jewellery from a deceased resident. They will hope that the relatives do not notice that these possibly valuable items have disappeared. If you remember and ask for them within a month or so, they will produce a small envelope containing the missing items and tell you that they were keeping them for you until you asked for them but that they didn't like to bother you with such an issue until you had recovered from the shock of bereavement. If you ask for the jewellery after a month or so, they will deny all knowledge of it.

# D

## DATING

If you are over 65 and dating, you can enjoy the fact that you are unlikely to have to meet your companion's parents.

## DEMENTIA

Dementia is one of the things that worry the elderly most. They should not be so concerned for two reasons.

First, it is nowhere near as common as the media and the Alzheimer charities suggest it is.

Second, despite the lies told by the Alzheimer charities, and repeated by sloppy journalists, most dementia is curable.

Read that last bit again: despite the lies told by self-serving charities and ill-informed journalists, most cases of dementia are curable.

The reluctance of the media to provide honest, objective advice about dementia is, I fear, a sign of the times.

Most daily newspapers in the UK carry stories about Alzheimer's (which is invariably confused with dementia) but their stories are usually a disgraceful mixture of hypothesis, self-promoting nonsense, rumour and myth. *The Daily Telegraph* and the *Daily Mail* seem to me to be the worst offenders. No newspapers have reported the simple but reassuring truth – that many alleged cases of dementia are reversible or treatable – lest this distract from their scaremongering, headline grabbing nonsenses.

The truth is that you should not worry unduly about dementia. It is a devastating problem but it is relatively uncommon and often curable.

Doctors and nurses and other health care professionals who tell you that it's never curable are stupid and ill informed and should be put into the stocks so that we can all throw rotten vegetables at them. They should then be fired.

As a matter of fact, the incidence of dementia among the elderly is around 7% and that is considerably lower than the incidence of insanity among 20 to 30-year-olds.

The incidence of dementia seems high because Alzheimer patients in particular tend to live fairly normal life spans and so there seem to be a lot of them about. (People don't die of Alzheimer's as is commonly reported. People who are suffering from Alzheimer's disease usually die of pneumonia or they are starved to death by hospital or nursing home staff. Tragically, this is not an exaggeration, it is a fact.)

So, what types of dementia can be cured?

First, there is the type of dementia caused by a disease called normal pressure hydrocephalus. Most doctors have never heard of this. Many specialists have never heard of it. But it is a major cause of dementia and it can be cured. (See the entry NORMAL PRESSURE HYDROCEPHALUS).

Second, there is the type of dementia caused by prescription drugs.

It is fact that many of the residents who reside in old folks' homes, rest homes and nursing homes are (with the cooperation of a bad doctor) sedated with prescription drugs. This is done to reduce the workload and to keep the place looking tidier. The elderly residents are also frequently encouraged to remain inactive and undemanding.

As a result, the incidence of dementia is vastly overestimated. Thousands of alleged Alzheimer sufferers would recovery in days if they were taken off their damned medication for it is a sad fact that the commonest cause of confusion in the elderly is not dementia but overmedication. Countless thousands have been drugged and the results of their drugging sometimes mimics Alzheimer's and sometimes creates Alzheimer's through disuse atrophy. Muscles atrophy if we don't use them and so does the brain.

There are many myths and confusions about dementia in general and Alzheimer's disease in particular. It is said that dementia is uncommon among smokers. This is true. But it is only true because most smokers die before the sort of age when dementia is likely. It is said that dementia is commoner among individuals who do not have loving families. If this is true it is because elderly individuals without loving families are likely to be living alone in a nursing home of some kind and likely therefore to be drugged into submission. I cannot stress sufficiently that many elderly patients who appear to be demented are, in fact, confused because they have been drugged with tranquillisers, sedatives or sleeping tablets. It is said that massive exposure to stress damages the brain in a way which makes dementia more likely. This is true.

You can safely ignore newspaper articles telling you that large quantities of curry, sherbet dip or candyfloss will prevent or cure Alzheimer's disease. These silly articles are written by ignorant journalists who should be encouraged to go bungee jumping without the rope.

Your chances of developing dementia can, however, be reduced by avoiding excess weight, dealing effectively with high blood pressure, stopping smoking, taking regular exercise, controlling diseases such as diabetes and maintaining social contact with other human beings.

However, the best way to prevent or delay or slow down dementia is to keep your brain active by writing your autobiography, learning a language, doing crossword puzzles, playing chess, backgammon or bridge, or working your way through a selection of brain teasers. This doesn't always work but it's the best known therapy and it has the advantage of sharpening the brain.

Finally, and I make no apology for repeating this, do not forget that a large number of patients who present with dementia, and who are misdiagnosed as suffering from Alzheimer's disease, are suffering from Normal Pressure Hydrocephalus which is curable with a fairly simple operation.

Oh, and one other thing: not being able to remember a name or two doesn't mean you're developing dementia. It's normal.


## DIGNITY

When you become older, you will find that your dignity is constantly under threat. You will be ignored, disrespected, humbled, humiliated and patronised.

To avoid these horrors you must be assertive. Object strongly if you hear phrases such 'old biddy', 'dirty old man', 'granny' or grandpa. These are the equivalent of calling someone a 'nigger' or a 'paki'.

Don't allow people to call you by your first name unless you want them to and are allowed and encouraged to call them by their first names. (I wrote a novel about a character called Mr Henry Mulligan who insists on being called 'Mister Mulligan'.)

The aged are venerable and entitled to be treated with esteem. This is a right.

The whole process of dehumanising is complex and commonplace.

For example, people (particularly in the health care businesses) who know that I am a doctor but retired often make a point of calling me Mr as though to make it clear that I am no longer a doctor. It is part of the studied humiliation of the elderly. I haven't lost my qualifications but I'm made to feel useless and irrelevant.

Well, they try.


# DISABILITY

Disability isn't a consequence of old age – it is a consequence of illness or accident. There are lots of old people who aren't disabled and there are lots of young people who are disabled.

The assumption that anyone who is over the age of 65 must also be disabled is a dangerous myth born of a marriage between ignorance and prejudice.

Road signs which warn motorists that elderly folk may be crossing the road, and then accompany the warnings with pictures of decrepit looking hunchbacks, are patronising and are doing a great disservice. They are perpetuating a dangerous prejudice which is easily turned into active discrimination.

Would anyone dare put up a sign saying 'Black people crossing'?

What are the chances of the council putting up a sign saying 'Gays crossing' or 'Beware transsexuals crossing'?

There would be rioting in the nation's universities and the celebrity twats on twitter would explode with outrage.

## DISCRIMINATION

Older citizens are oppressed, ignored and discriminated against. There can be no doubt that discrimination against the elderly is the last remaining stronghold occupied by the prejudiced and the bigoted. Discrimination against individuals on the basis of skin colour, sex or religion has long been considered unpleasant, indefensible and illegal. But discrimination against the elderly is commonplace and entirely legal.

Some of the ways in which the elderly are discriminated against are, arguably, well-intentioned. They are, however, still examples of discrimination.

Colleges which offer special classes in computing skills, art or languages for the elderly probably did so in the belief that they are providing a valuable service.

But I wonder if they would feel so pleased with themselves if they offered special classes for blacks, Jews, homosexuals or women?

Can you imagine the outcry if a college advertised an introductory class in computing exclusively for homosexual students?

The elderly are neither stupid nor slow and those who wish to study a subject can manage just as well, thank you very much, in a class organised for everyone.

Some publishers fall into the same trap – offering special books on computing for the elderly. The very idea of publishing books on general subjects especially for the elderly is invariably and inevitably patronising.

Can you imagine seeing a poster advertising college classes: 'The Special Computer Class for Jews Will Start When the Art Class for Homosexuals Has Finished.'

Some even more toxic forms of discrimination are commonplace.

First, and most notably, is the commonplace requirement that individuals retire from work when they reach a certain, arbitrarily selected, age. There are laws against age discrimination but they are observed about as strictly as the laws requiring dogs to be kept on leads in public places – that it is to say they are not observed at all.

Second, there is the discrimination against those drivers who have reached an age which the authorities decide, without any evidentiary justification, requires that an individual lose their licence or be required to take an additional test. This example of discrimination can cause enormous hardship. The evidence shows quite clearly, of course, that the authorities would reduce accidents on the road far more effectively if they were to ban anyone under the age of 25 from driving at all. (Anyone looking for evidence for this could simply look at the fact that insurance companies, not known to act without the support of reliable evidence, invariably charge reduced premiums for elderly drivers and increased premiums for younger drivers.)

Third, it is probably not widely known, but NHS staff frequently make decisions about which patients will be saved and which will be allowed to die. The elderly come at the bottom of the list when decisions like this are being made.

This is a lethal form of discrimination.

The problem is that because of all the money spent on administration and used in providing non-essential treatments, there simply aren't enough resources to provide for everyone in genuine need. The rules which have to be followed mean that people with children take precedence over people who don't have children. So a scrounger who has never done a day's work in his life, but who has 12 kids, will take precedence over someone who works hard, pays taxes and plays an important role in society. The sensible and hard-working always lose out in every conceivable way. I have a vision that before long, the NHS will introduce a reality television programme called *Who lives? Who dies? You decide?*. Twelve patients needing kidney transplants will all take part in the programme and 'sell' themselves to the audience. The winner will receive the transplant and the NHS will keep all the phone line money. The awful, awful thing is that I cannot convince myself it could not happen.

# DISEASE

Wobbly or unstable 70-year-olds don't wobble because they are old. They wobble or are unstable because there is something wrong with them. Not all old people wobble or are unstable but some young people do wobble and are unstable.

It is sometimes said that very few diseases are exclusive to the elderly but actually there are none.

So, for example, hearing and vision problems can arise at any age – though the confidence tricksters flogging hearing aids target the elderly because they tend to be lonely, nervous and gullible.

What a great business model that is.

# DOCTORS

Family doctors often boast that they specialise in women's problems or paediatrics (and this is especially true now that so many of the doctors are women) but very, very few family doctors express a special interest in caring for the elderly.

Indeed, it is a sad fact that too many doctors now seem convinced that anyone over 70 isn't really worth treating, though the vast majority can live good, productive, useful lives, and contribute a great deal more to society than they already have.

Doctors dislike elderly patients for a variety reasons.

First and foremost, of course, they dislike the elderly because they have been taught to dislike the elderly. In the UK, the official government policy is to kill off as many old people as possible. In hospitals this is done, with official approval, by withholding food, drink and potentially life-saving medication. Since GPs are trained in hospitals, it is hardly surprising that they carry this prejudice with them when they become family practitioners.

Many young GPs also dislike elderly patients because they fear they will be a nuisance and take up a disproportionate amount of time. (This fear should be, but is not, assuaged by the fact that the Government pays GPs more money for looking after older patients than it pays them for looking after young patients).

Doctors also dislike the old because they fear they may die even when they are being treated and therefore reinforce the fear that the doctor herself is incompetent in some way.

And, of course, doctors don't like patients who die because every death is a reminder that we are all mortal and that however important we are, life always leads inexorably towards death.

Have absolutely nothing to do with doctors who tell you that you are 'lucky to be around' or who ask 'what do you expect at your age'? when you ask them for advice.

Finally, here are four ways in which GPs can make huge amounts of extra money by exploiting their patients:

**By over diagnosing**
Doctors receive huge extra fees if they diagnose patients as suffering from particular health problems such as dementia. Be careful not to allow your doctor to label you as suffering from disorders such as COPD (Chronic Obstructive Pulmonary Disease). The doctor may fill his wallet with extra cash but you risk carrying a possibly inaccurate label with you for life. And once you are labelled, doctors will want to give you drugs you may not need. The drug companies love this. But the unnecessary drugs may kill you.

**By vaccinating**
Doctors receive massive fees for vaccinating patients. And they get additional huge fees for reaching official vaccination targets. Many doctors 'push' vaccines on patients so that they can make more money. It is common for nurses to give the jabs and doctors to pocket the fees. Doctors now routinely target patients with letters advocating vaccination. Some doctors even threaten to withhold essential treatment from patients who refuse vaccination. And yet anyone who claims all vaccines are safe and effective is lying.

**By using patients as drug company guinea pigs**
Doctors can earn big money by doing 'trials' for drug companies. If your doctor gives you drugs that don't need a prescription – and asks you back to the surgery for frequent check- ups – then you are

probably being used as a guinea pig for a new drug. You may be happy about this. But your doctor should tell you what is happening. Most don't. And remember most new drugs are merely commercial variations on existing drugs which work perfectly well. You may be taking health risks for no advantage to you or anyone else.

**By accepting too many drug company gifts**
Look around: if your doctor's surgery and reception area are littered with promotional pens, mugs and other free gifts then your doctor may be spending too much time with drug company reps – and her or his prescribing habits may have been influenced by the salesperson. Good doctors get their prescribing information from journals and lectures and do not waste time seeing drug company sales reps.

# DRUGS

Most doctors are obsessed with drug therapy. Many don't seem to have heard of the variety of effective non-drug solutions which now exist. If it doesn't come in a blister pack and isn't packaged by one of the world's big drug companies, they don't believe it can possibly do any good.

Drug companies need to be regarded with great scepticism for they are (together with the food and tobacco industries) one of the three major modern threats to human health.

The fact is that patients and drug companies have diametrically opposed interests. The patient wants to get better. But the drug company will make bigger profits if the patient remains ill – and continues to need to take drugs. Doctors have sold out to the drug industry and they have (as I pointed out almost half a century ago) become little more than a marketing arm of the world's most profitable industry.

Here are a few things all patients should know about prescription drugs:

1) Drug companies have, not surprisingly, welcomed and taken advantage of the medical profession's collective stupidity, greed and naivety. They have virtually taken over postgraduate medical education. Their advertising dominates medical journals. And as a result, most doctors (not just the bad ones) are obsessed with drugs because they simply aren't aware that there are other ways to deal with health problems.

2) A survey of over 2,000 patients admitted to hospital showed that within a ten year period, the number of drugs prescribed per patient had shown an increase of almost 50%. Today it is hard to avoid the conclusion that medicine is run for the benefit of large drug companies which make fortunes out of persuading gullible doctors to prescribe useless drugs. Persuading ill-informed doctors (and ignorant nurses who have demanded and been given the authority to prescribe) to prescribe their wretched products is a highly profitable business.

3) Most of the drugs which are prescribed have never been properly tested or proved to be of any use. The evidence for this apparently provocative claim can be found in books of mine such as *How To Stop Your Doctor Killing You* and *Betrayal of Trust*. Even drug treatments which are well established have still not yet been properly evaluated. For example, doctors still don't know whether a course of antibiotics should be given for five, seven, ten or fourteen days for the best results. How many doctors know that new drugs are tested and licensed for safety (in a vague, entirely satisfactory sort of way it has to be said) but not for effectiveness?

4) Drugs are wildly overprescribed, both by hospital doctors and by general practitioners. It is now nearly 50 years since I first exposed the dangers of benzodiazepines and 30 years since a government admitted that it had introduced new legislation as a result of my campaign. But still benzodiazepines are overprescribed and still they are prescribed badly, without thought and without awareness of the often disastrous consequences for patients. Vast numbers of other drugs, including antibiotics and painkillers as well as antidepressants, are overprescribed.

5) Most doctors are so under the spell of the drug industry that they steadfastly and stubbornly refuses to acknowledge that 'alternative' or 'complementary' medical techniques have a great deal to offer. Gentle therapies, and gentle practitioners, are deliberately demonised by the drug industry controlled medical establishment. Orthodox doctors routinely lie about the value of alternative medicines. Anyone who says that alternative therapy never works for cancer, for example, is either very stupid, a sadist or simply woefully ill-informed. Or, most likely receiving a large grant or fee from a drug company.

6) A reader wrote to say that her late husband was a pharmacist for over 60 years. She said that although his daily job was dispensing medicines, he always preferred to use natural remedies himself. He was, she said, amazed at the length of time patients were kept on some drugs without any check to find out if they still needed them.

7) Even universities are now very closely linked to drug companies. Since 1988, British universities have been allowed to exploit the intellectual property they generate. As a result, academics around the world have become multimillionaires through working on new drugs while accepting university salaries. They and the drug companies then make fortunes out of the work done with taxpayers' money. Astonishingly, 45 out of the world's 50 top selling drugs were developed and or tested with taxpayers' money. So many academics have links to drug companies that there are now virtually no independent scientists in Britain. Corruption is embedded and endemic.

8) Every patient who takes a drug – even a well-tried drug – is participating in an experiment. Most doctors either do not understand this or they forget it in the heat of daily practice.

9) Doctors often prescribe several drugs at once; frequently prescribing two drugs which interact dangerously. The dangers of polypharmacy still fail to be recognised, even though interactions are common and can be deadly. Mixing common prescription drugs could kill and might exacerbate serious health problems such as dementia. I have been warning for many years that drug interactions

are dangerous and deadly. In my book *The Medicine Men* (first published in 1975) I wrote: 'It is the problem of drug interactions which is likely to cause most controversy in the future. There are many possibilities. Metabolism of one drug may affect another. Drugs may react chemically together within the body and excretory rates may be modified with devastating results. Patent medicines and even foodstuffs may react.'

10) The drug industry has convinced doctors that everyone they see must need a drug and that there is a pill for every ill. The majority of doctors might as well be employed directly by the drug companies as pretend to be independent, authoritative scientists. They prescribe what they are told to prescribe in exactly the same way that the drug company representatives promote what they are told to promote. The fact that the medical profession is dominated and controlled by the pharmaceutical industry would not matter so much if the drug industry were honest, responsible and ethical. But it isn't. According to a survey published in the *Annals of Internal Medicine* nearly two thirds of the pharmaceutical advertisements in medical journals were either grossly misleading or downright inaccurate. A total of 109 advertisements from 10 leading medical journals were each reviewed by two doctors and an academic clinical pharmacist. The reviewers used guidelines from the Food and Drug Administration to assess the advertisements. In 30% of cases, the independent reviewers disagreed with the advertiser's claim that the drug was the drug of choice. In 44% of cases, the reviewers thought that the advertisement would lead to improper prescribing if a doctor had no information about the drug other than that provided in the advertisement.

11) New diseases are 'discovered' all the time. You will excuse my cynicism, and my suspicion that these new diseases are discovered for a reason, when I tell you that most of these new diseases just happen to be enormously profitable. One of the most profitable is a disorder known as COPD (chronic obstructive pulmonary disease) which is actually a relatively new catch all name for a variety of chest disorders including asthma, emphysema and chronic bronchitis. In the bad old days, patients with these individual disorders were treated as and when treatment was required. Today, the new philosophy seems to be that patients with COPD should take

constant medication – whether they actually need it or not. Another new disease is 'isolated systolic hypertension'. Just a few years ago, doctors believed that only the diastolic figure was of significance when measuring blood pressure. The systolic, or higher figure, was regarded as of little consequence by itself. And then drug companies noticed that around 80% of all individuals over the age of 65 had normal diastolic pressures but systolic pressures that were high compared with younger patients. And so, surprise, surprise, a new disease came into being – 'isolated systolic hypertension' – and it became necessary for doctors to start treating the high systolic pressure.

12) Every doctor and every patient should remember that drug companies do not want to see patients cured or illness conquered. The drug industry wants to see as many people as possible suffering from long-term, incurable illnesses. The politicians want to see people die before they become old and dependant. If more money was spent on preventing cancer (around 80% of cancers are preventable and other diseases) then the average life expectancy would go up dramatically and the incidence of disease and disability would fall. But the drug industry doesn't want a healthy nation (it would sell fewer drugs) and the politicians don't want any more people living to an old age because they know that they would not be able to cope with the pension bills they would have to pay. The astonishing truth is that the drug industry needs to keep the voters ill in order to maintain its profits and the politicians want to help them achieve that aim. Drug companies do not want patients to be healed. Sick people are profitable. Healthy people are not. Turning people into chronic invalids is far more profitable than curing them.

13) Drug making is so crude that Severin Schwan the boss of Roche, the massive and powerful Swiss drugs firm which made a fortune out of benzodiazepines has said: 'Drugmaking is so crude that half of all known diseases cannot be treated at all, and the drugs for the other half work properly only half the time and with huge side effects.' Good to know. Every doctor should have those words engraved on his forehead.

14) There isn't a drug on the planet which can't do harm – and even kill people. It's the risk-benefit relationship which doctors (and patients) ignore. If a doctor gives you a drug without which you will die then the risks are almost inconsequential. But if you don't really need a drug and the drug makes you ill then the risk is unacceptable. Antibiotics save lives. But they also kill people. If you have an infection which might kill you then taking an antibiotic is a good thing. But if you have a viral infection then taking an antibiotic (which might kill you) is pretty stupid. There's no benefit but a lot of risk. Some drugs are potentially useful. All drugs are potentially harmful.

15) Most people take far too many medicines – without knowing why they are taking them, what the medicine is designed to do, what the side effects might be and what might happen if the drug is not taken. Doctors have created generalised drug dependency among patients. The business of handing out drugs has become a part of the consultation ritual. When a doctor doesn't have the foggiest idea what to do, she reaches for the prescription pad. And, of course, many doctors use the prescription pad as a way to cut short a consultation. Not surprisingly, doctor-induced illness is now a major problem. It may often be easier to end a consultation by handing over a prescription or a medicine. But that doesn't mean that it is the right thing to do. On the contrary, doctors should be more responsible for this. They should educate their patients and they should only prescribe drugs when drugs are essential, useful and likely to do more harm than good.

16) Sadly, doctors know very little about the medicines they recommend to their patients. Most of the information they have comes directly from the company selling the product – which obviously has a vested interest in promoting the virtues and covering up the defects.

17) Since the end of the 1970s, I have argued that we need an international computerised drug monitoring service – designed to make sure that doctors in one part of the world know when doctors in other countries have spotted problems. Astonishingly, no such system exists. You might imagine that when a drug is withdrawn in

one country other countries will take similar action. But you would be wrong. One drug that was officially withdrawn from the market in the USA and France was not officially withdrawn in the UK until five years later.

18) The majority of illnesses do not need drug treatment. Most patients who visit a doctor neither want nor expect drug treatment. But at least eight out of ten patients who visit a general practitioner will be given a prescription (though growing numbers of patients do not take the drugs that are prescribed for them).

19) It is now widely accepted that at least 40% of all the people who are given prescription medicines will suffer uncomfortable, hazardous or potentially lethal side effects. And yet the vast majority of doctors never admit that their patients suffer any side effects. In Britain, for example, five out of six doctors have never reported any drug side effects to the authorities – authorities who admit that they receive information on no more than 10% - 15% of even the most serious adverse drug reactions occurring in patients. In other words, they admit that they never hear about at least 85% - 90% of all dangerous drug reactions. It is even accepted that some doctors will withhold reports of serious adverse reactions, and keep their suspicions to themselves, in the hope that they may later be able to win fame by publishing their findings in a journal or revealing their discovery to a newspaper or magazine. There is a free list of possible side effects for many of the most popular prescription drugs on my website www.vernoncoleman.com).

20) Ironically, although we consume greater and greater quantities of medicine than ever before, more of us are ill today than at any time in history. On any day you care to choose in just about any developed country you care to mention over half the population will be taking a drug of some kind. A survey of 9,000 Britons concluded that one in three people suffers from a long-standing illness or disability. Other surveys have shown that in any one 14 day period, 95% of the population consider themselves to be unwell for at least a few of those days. At no time in history has illness been so commonplace. We spend more than ever on health care but no one could argue that there is any less suffering in our society.

21) The medical profession, the drug industry and the regulatory bodies all accept that the hazards of using any particular drug will only be known when the drug has been given to large numbers of patients for a considerable period of time. But no one monitors drugs which are given and it is only when a problem becomes truly widespread that anyone notices.

22) In October 2008, it was finally admitted that taking aspirin to prevent heart attacks might do more harm than good. Prior to that date, many doctors were recommending that healthy patients took daily aspirin as a prophylactic. But there was never any convincing evidence showing that taking daily aspirin was wise. I had been so alarmed by the early research that I warned the instant it was published that the evidence didn't prove taking aspirin routinely was either safe or effective. My advice was ignored and sneered at but you have to ask yourself who benefitted most from the suggestion that vast numbers of healthy people should take a daily drug? Sir Richard Doll, who did some research on this issue, was, like many members of the medical establishment, later discredited. After his death, it was revealed that he, like so many other eminent doctors, had received consultancy payments from chemical companies whose products he had defended. For example, he received $1,500 a day from Monsanto (one of the world's most disgusting companies) and had a 'relationship' with them from 1976 until 2002. Pity we weren't told this when the miserable bastard was alive. All doctors should have to declare publicly any money or gifts they have received from drug or other companies.

23) In Britain, doctors are not allowed to prescribe drugs for serious health problems which exclusively affect the elderly but they are allowed to spend untold hundreds of millions on infertility, cosmetic surgery and sex change operations – all of which are optional and none of which are life threatening problems.

# E

## EMPLOYMENT

Sensible employers realise that older folk make better and more reliable employees. Statistics show that older employees have less time off work, are involved in fewer accidents and have fewer disabling injuries. Older employees work harder, their productivity is better and they are less likely to spend all the time tweeting, faffing around with their Facebook page or complaining that the company policy in 1871 was demeaning to one-legged Lithuanians. Older employees are unlikely to become pregnant or to need time off work because their kids' teachers are on strike. A growing number of employers, particularly those running small businesses, realise that employing a woman of child bearing age is like sitting on a time bomb. If you hire someone who turns out to be pregnant then she can take a year off work and the employer is not allowed to replace her. So that's another reason for hiring older folk. It is sometimes assumed that only geniuses, judges and politicians can continue to work after the age of 65. This is bollocks. The elderly are more likely to be useful and effective than any other group. Old people, like old cars, are more interesting. They can be enormously rewarding and maintenance costs in the long run are usually much lower.

## EUTHANASIA

Euthanasia (sometimes admitted and sometimes not) is now commonly practised. The elderly are invariably the victims.

For many years in the UK, doctors and nurses were encouraged to follow something called the Liverpool Care Pathway. This was a murderers' charter, which allowed doctors and nurses to withhold food, water and essential treatment from patients who were over 65 and who are, therefore, regarded as an expensive and entirely disposable nuisance. The Liverpool Care Pathway is being replaced by something called Sustainable Development Goals (which originated with the United Nations).

Sustainable Development Goals allows the NHS to discriminate against anyone over the age of 70 on the grounds that people who die when they are over 70 cannot be said to have died 'prematurely' and so will not count when the nation's healthcare is being assessed.

Governments everywhere love this new rule because it gives the State permission to get rid of citizens who are of pensionable age and, therefore, regarded by society's accountants as a 'burden'.

It was back in February 2005 that it was revealed that the Government had advised that hospital patients with little hope of recovery should be allowed to die because of the cost of keeping them alive. The key words were 'little hope of recovery'. Who says?

The Labour Government responsible for this wicked nonsense suggested that 'old people' be denied the right to food and water if they fell into a coma or couldn't speak for themselves. So much for any hope for stroke victims.

The Government suggested that the need to cut costs came before the need to preserve the lives of patients and decided it had the right to overturn a right-to-life ruling which had been made when a judge ordered that artificial nutrition and hydration should not be withdrawn unless the life of a patient could be described as 'intolerable'. (The judge had added that when there was any doubt, preservation of life should take precedence.)

Of course, depriving the elderly of food and water is sometimes more a consequence of incompetence than official policy. When my mother was in hospital in Exeter, she couldn't feed herself but the staff didn't feed her. If no relative could get to the hospital to feed her she didn't eat. Drinks were put on her tray and then taken away untouched. 'Not thirsty, today?' an idiot would ask merrily as she whisked away the still full cup.

Meanwhile, the Government pours money into subsidising the lives of the lazy and the work-shy. Healthy 30-year-olds sit around growing chip backsides and beer bellies, slumped in front of their high definition digital television sets and opening the windows to let the heat out because it's easier than turning down the central heating.

The elderly are classified as the 'Unwanted Generation': they are a political embarrassment. Elderly individuals facing blindness from age-related macular disease are denied drugs that might have prevented their blindness because they are considered expensive, useless and expendable. The theory is that they don't contribute and rarely vote and can, therefore, be disregarded.

But those who believe this will be old sooner than they think. And the definition of 'old' is getting younger by the year.

How have we managed to forget that in the 1930s, the Nazis deliberately starved and dehydrated elderly and vulnerable patients because they were regarded as a useless burden on society? That is exactly what we are doing today.

Actually, we are probably worse than the Nazis.

Today, some doctors and general purpose campaigners with Twitter accounts and Facebook pages want to be able to kill people off when they are dying, decrepit, expensive, unable to complete an Iron Man Triathalon or in a great deal of pain.

Others, however, worry about making killing legal.

I'm one of the worriers. I can see all sorts of problems.

The Government has already given doctors the legal right to kill old people (by starving them to death, or depriving them of fluids) if they are filling a hospital bed that the administrators want to use for a patient requiring cosmetic surgery or infertility treatment.

I can now see the Government taking advantage of a euthanasia law to get rid of all sorts of patients with chronic or potentially expensive illnesses; assisted dying will metamorphose into something quite different to the gentle and kindly easing which more civilised proponents envisage.

If a euthanasia law is introduced, it will mark the return of the death penalty.

But this time we won't be killing the possibly guilty; we will be killing the definitely innocent.

The world is full of people who are still breathing and living full lives despite having been diagnosed as being terminally ill.

So, for example, I heard not long ago about a doctor in County Antrim, Northern Ireland who was wrongly diagnosed with terminal cancer and told to prepare for death. She was told that she had three months to live. Fortunately, being a doctor, the patient discharged herself, went to a London hospital and was diagnosed as having gallstones.

Twenty five years ago, I myself was diagnosed as having kidney cancer and told I had six months to live. I thought a little and made a new diagnosis. I had irritable bowel syndrome.

It wouldn't be difficult to fill a large book with such stories.

When I was a GP, I saw a number of patients who lived far longer than seemed possible – often because they had a very good reason not to die. So, for example, I remember seeing a patient who was the wife of an alcoholic playwright and the mother of two teenage children. She had breast cancer but refused to die until her children had grown up. She had secondaries in just about every organ in her body but still she wouldn't die. I remember sending a sample of her blood to the laboratory to be tested. They rang me up and asked me what I was playing at. They said that no one could be alive with the blood readings they'd taken. But she was alive. And she lived for several more years. I just stopped taking blood samples because there wasn't any point.

## EXERCISE

Take regular exercise. In a study for the American Administration on Ageing, a class of 70-year-old men joined a one year exercise programme and after the twelve months they had the bodily reactions of 40-year-old men.

## EXPERTS

Far too much faith is put in experts. I have lost count of the number of times experts have told me something was possible (when it turned out not to be) or, more commonly, impossible (when it turned out to be). And doctors can be wrong as often as car mechanics, plumbers, surveyors, lawyers, dentists and central heating engineers.

When my mother was ill in the teaching hospital in Exeter, she was seen by nine specialists. They all missed the diagnosis – even though my wife and I repeatedly suggested the diagnosis which turned out to be the correct one.

When my father was ill, doctors prescribed a drug which I warned would kill him. Nurses then ignored my advice and insisted on giving him the drug which had been so foolishly prescribed. He was predictably dead within 24 hours.

# F

## FALLS

Most falls take place in the home and are a result of simple, obvious hazards which could have been avoided. Don't go out in the snow or ice unless you have spikes fitted to the bottoms of your shoes. Carry a cane if you are in the slightest bit wobbly. (A cane is also useful for getting rid of annoying dogs or menacing youths. Make the first blow a hard one.)

Make sure that your bath has a grab handle and a non-slip mat. Make sure that rugs are firmly fixed and that there are no carpet edges sticking up waiting to trip you. Equip your home with handles at difficult positions (e.g. at the top of the stairs). Put handrails around your garden to give you a little support when you are examining the hollyhocks. Make sure that dark corners of your house or driveway are well lit. If possible, have two lights in particularly dark lobbies so that if one bulb goes the remaining bulb will still be lit. Keep torches around the house and carry a small one with you at all times. Doing all of this (or having it done for you) will cost far less than a week in a nursing home. Go through your home looking for booby traps – it is one of the most useful things you can do to help yourself survive.

Not long ago, American doctors noticed that an increasing number of elderly citizens were falling. No one seemed able to understand the phenomenon.

The same thing has been noticed in Britain. More and more elderly patients are falling and breaking bones.

I've been standing at the back of the room waving my arms in the air but no one has taken any notice.

I know what the problem is.

I know what the solution is.

These elderly patients have a condition called 'normal pressure hydrocephalus'.

I believe that the Alzheimer industry is helping to suppress the truth because those involved want the words 'Alzheimer's' and 'dementia' to be synonymous.

(Many health problems have spawned industries. There is a cancer industry. And an AIDS industry. And there is now an Alzheimer's industry.)

The fact is that normal pressure hydrocephalus is, for example, commoner than Parkinson's disease. It is one of the commonest causes of dementia. And it is curable with a simple, cheap operation.

Meanwhile, thousands of elderly folk who could be cured are falling and breaking bones. Falling is the first symptom for normal pressure hydrocephalus. Dementia comes next.

I have been exposing medical scandals for decades.

Believe me when I tell you that this is the biggest medical scandal of our time. And no one seems to give a damn. Why? That's simple. Because the people involved are elderly.


# FEAR

The elderly tend to be prone to more fears than any other group in our society. This is partly because the elderly often feel physically vulnerable but it is mainly because they are old enough to know that, as P.G.Wodehouse put it so colourfully in his novel *Uneasy Money*, life is nothing but a series of sharp corners, 'round each of which Fate lies in wait for us with a stuffed eel-skin'?

Here are the top ten fears common among the elderly:

1) Memory – Losing their memory, their marbles and their ability to know whether today is Tuesday or a wheelbarrow. This fear results largely from scare campaigns run by newspapers and charities dealing with Alzheimer's Disease. The newspaper editors can be forgiven since they're desperately trying to compete with the internet and sell copies of their failing rags. But the charities are less easily excused. They just want to raise more money for bigger salaries and fatter pensions.

2) Poverty – Finding themselves trapped and imprisoned in a rotten nursing home where the staff were trained by graduates from the Dachau School of Auxiliary Nursing.

3) Ill health.

4) Being robbed or mugged.

5) Loneliness.

6) Falling over and breaking something.

7) Being a burden.

8) Losing their dignity

9) Being trapped in a fire.

Look at your life and try to find ways to tackle these fears. So, for example, it is a good idea to make sure that you have an escape route planned if there is a fire.

## FLUIDS

You would be horrified if you knew how many elderly folk die because they don't drink enough. Your body needs fluid more than it needs food. Without an adequate supply of liquid your blood will thicken, your kidneys will pack up, your heart will be overworked and you will stand a much greater chance of dying. It is obviously particularly important to ensure that your fluid intake is adequate when the weather is warm. You can easily tell whether you are drinking enough merely by studying the colour of your urine. If it has a definite yellowish colouring then you need to drink more. And if you aren't producing urine as often as usual then you need to drink more as a matter of urgency.

# FOOD

It's not what you eat that matters but how many calories you devour. Around 30% of the people you know will die not of cancer or heart disease or a stroke but of overeating.

Eating too much means that you age faster and earlier.

It has been known since 1930 that the best way to slow down the ageing process is to cut your calorie intake.

Why don't people tell you this? Because governments and doctors don't want you to live longer.

Most of the damage to your health is done by what you eat long before you reach old age. But eating too much food and putting on excess weight will lead directly to health problems, reduced mobility and a shorter lifespan.

Remember, remember that your government wants you to die soon because then you will be less of a nuisance. Never forget this when you see and hear the government giving out health advice.

More cancer is caused by food than tobacco and nearly all the cancers are caused by just one food: meat. The same foodstuff is also largely responsible for the high incidence of circulatory disease – including heart attacks and strokes.

There is clear medical and scientific evidence available to show that nothing, not even tobacco, influences your chances of developing cancer as much as the food you choose to eat. It is estimated that between 30% and 60% of all cancers are caused by what you eat.

Doctors, scientists and supporters of the cancer industry (all of whom realise that there is no money to be made out of preventing cancer, but tons of loot to be made out of doing research and flogging 'cures' and treatments) merrily ignore this fact and claim that the battle against cancer will only be won with the aid of more money. They claim that in order to obtain the information we need we must spend, spend, spend.

But that isn't true.

It is not more knowledge we need (we have, as I pointed out in *Paper Doctors* nearly 40 years ago, already amassed far more knowledge than we will ever use in our lifetime), but the ability and courage and determination to use the knowledge we already have.

And the evidence proving that certain types of food cause cancer and premature death has been available for a remarkably long time.

Amazingly, it has for many years been widely agreed that 80% of all cancers are preventable – using knowledge which we have available at the moment. In other words, ignorance (sustained through political and industrial expediency) is responsible for 80% of the millions of deaths caused by cancer each year. And much of that ignorance involves the effect that food has upon the health.

Way back in 1981, it was estimated that dietary modifications might result in a one third reduction in the number of deaths from cancer in the United States with a 90% reduction in deaths from cancer of the stomach and large bowel; a 50% reduction in deaths from cancers of the endometrium, gallbladder, pancreas and breast; a 20% reduction in deaths from cancers of the lung, larynx, bladder, cervix, mouth, pharynx and oesophagus and a 10% reduction in deaths from other sites.

Back in 1982, the National Research Council in the United States of America published a technical report entitled *Diet, Nutrition and Cancer* which showed that diet was probably the single most important factor in the development of cancer, and, even then, 30 years ago, that there was evidence linking cancers of the breast, colon and prostate to particular foods or types of food.

It is a scandal of astonishing proportions that a majority of the population still does not know about these vitally important and well-established links. It is an even bigger scandal that most doctors still dismiss the idea of a food/cancer link as mumbo-jumbo nonsense, preferring to rely entirely on prescription drugs, radiotherapy and surgery as 'treatments' for cancer. The average medical student spends more time staring down a microscope at histology slides than he or she spends studying nutrition.

Today, it is an undeniable fact that you can dramatically reduce your chances of developing cancer of the breast, cancer of the prostate, cancer of the colon, cancer of the ovary or cancer of the uterus by not eating meat. And yet when I checked one large (over 1,000 pages long) medical textbook, I found that the chapter on cancer summed up the role of food as a causal agent in just one, rather short, sentence.

I find this all extremely difficult to understand. I have been studying scientific research papers for over half a century and I have never seen such convincing research as that which shows the links between particular types of food and particular types of cancer. I have absolutely no doubt that if these undeniable links had been properly publicised, countless millions of lives could – and would – have been saved. The suppression of this information by a greedy and conscience-free food industry, compliant, revenue conscious politicians, a cancer industry dominated by grant-hungry researchers and an uncaring, drug company dominated medical profession has, I sincerely believe, led to more deaths than any war in history.

Since the early 1980s, the amount of evidence linking diet to cancer has grown steadily. In 1990, even the British Medical Association, hardly an organisation which would be widely described as revolutionary, supported the view that there is a link between food and cancer. Their published view was that 35% of cancers are caused by the natural constituents of food and that another 1 per cent of cancers are caused by food additives.

Other organisations suggest that the link between food and cancer is even higher. The National Academy of Sciences in the United States, founded in 1863 by Act of Congress to serve as an official adviser to the US Government in all matters of science and technology, has reported that researchers have estimated that almost 60% of women's cancers and a little more than 40% of men's cancers are related to nutritional factors. (Readers who want to see more evidence proving that meat causes cancer will find it in my book *Food for Thought* which contains details of 26 scientific papers proving the link.)

The evidence linking meat eating to illness and death is incontestable. Meat eaters have three times the risk of developing diabetes, compared with vegans. Red and processed meats are clearly linked to colon cancer and other forms of the disease. And of course meat products are often contaminated with faecal bacteria, leading to deadly infections. (Meat products may include bits of chopped up animal cancer as well as animal bowels – complete with the faeces inside.)

Consumption of red and processed meats increases the risks of bladder cancer too. A study of over 300,000 men and women found that those who consumed the most red meat had a 22% increased risk of bladder cancer, compared with those who ate the least.

Consumption of nitrites and nitrates (substances used for preserving, colouring and flavouring processed meats) was associated with a 28% to 29% increased risk. The study, in the journal *Cancer* was conducted as part of the *NIH-AARP Diet and Health Study*.

And eating meat leads to weight gain. The *American Journal of Clinical Nutrition* published a study involving 373,803 participants in the *European Prospective Investigation into Cancer* study. Those who ate 8.8 ounces of meat per day, gained more weight year by year, compared with people who ate less meat or none at all. The researchers concluded that reducing meat consumption may help people avoid weight gain. Girls who eat the most meat products during childhood may have an earlier onset of puberty, increasing their risks of diseases such as cancer, heart disease and osteoporosis. Researchers followed 3,298 girls in Bristol, England and found that 49% of girls who ate more than 12 portions of meat per week started their periods by the age of 12, compared with 35% of girls who ate fewer than four portions of meat per week.

It is, therefore, hardly surprising that the incidence of cancer is rising rapidly and is going to continue to rise. The main cause of cancer in Britain today is not the smoking of cigarettes but the eating of meat.

Not surprisingly, doctors (much of whose education is controlled by the pharmaceutical industry and a Government controlled by the pharmaceutical industry) prefer to deal with the problems created by meat eating by prescribing drugs. Drugs are always the treatment of choice these days for a profession which is owned needle, syringe and pen by the pharmaceutical industry.

(As an aside, it seems strange to me that doctors seem totally uninterested in the fact that feeding people meat is directly responsible for a number of the world's serious problems. First, animals need to be fed grain and if people stopped eating meat there would be plenty of food to go round. The millions starving to death could be fed. Second, growing all the grain needed to feed animals creates havoc for the environment. For example, it takes a million gallons of water to grow just one acre of corn to feed to cattle. And as the water trickles into streams and rivers, it carries with it the remains of the fertilisers the farmers used. The fertiliser chemicals pollute the water we drink (as I reported half a lifetime ago it is impossible to remove the chemicals from our drinking water). The fertiliser also makes algae overgrow in our rivers and as the algae decomposes it uses up oxygen in the water, killing the fish. In America, farmers are responsible for the existence of a 8,000 square mile dead zone below Louisiana and Texas. And, of course the 100 million cows in the USA are all belching out methane – which is much more potent as a greenhouse gas than carbon dioxide. But doctors don't worry about any of this stuff. And nor, indeed, do the climate change conspiracy theory loonies who believe that man-made climate change is the biggest threat to mankind.)

Incidentally, food doesn't just *cause* cancer.

It can help stop you recovering too.

However careful you are to avoid potentially cancerous chemicals, cancer cells will occasionally develop inside your body. Most of the time those cancer cells are dealt with speedily and effectively by your body's defence systems. White blood cells find and destroy cancer cells in just the same way that they find and destroy bacteria.

However, your body's natural immune system (and its ability to deal with cancer) will be damaged if you eat the wrong sort of foods – and will be aided and improved if you eat the right foods.

Fatty foods will weaken your immune system and make your body less capable of fighting off those occasional cancer cells. When researchers studied the blood of human volunteers they found that a low fat diet greatly improved the activity of the body's natural killer cells.

Amazingly, depressingly, cancer specialists and cancer charity workers still don't seem to understand or accept the importance of a healthy immune system in fighting cancer. (As far as the body's immune system is concerned, vegetable fats are just as bad as animal fats. In order to protect yourself against cancer you need to reduce your entire fat consumption – and that includes vegetable oils.)

Vegetarians have more than double the cancer cell destroying capability of non-vegetarians. But this is not entirely due to the low fat content of a vegetarian diet. It is probably also due to the fact that vegetarians consume fewer toxic chemicals and no animal proteins. And vegetarians have another advantage too: the ability of the human body's natural, killer cells to do their work is improved by substances such as beta-carotene which are found in considerable quantities in vegetables. (One survey of meat eaters showed that many could neither name nor describe any green vegetables).

Food provides us with the building blocks we need to grow and to stay alive. If we don't eat the right food we fall ill. If we are ill and don't eat the right food, we won't get well. Most people know this. Most people, that is, except the people who work in hospitals. The doctors, the nurses, the cooks, the dieticians and the administrators either don't know or don't care.

The food in hospitals is diabolical and contributes enormously to the death rate among patients. It seems rather crazy to give hospital patients a food item (meat) that is known to cause cancer. Sadly, most nutritionists, dieticians and chefs employed by hospitals are woefully ignorant about food. I don't expect chefs to know anything much about food but dieticians and nutritionists who fail to warn patients that eating meat causes cancer are either stupid or ignorant and should be fired and retrained as lavatory attendants. Hospitals which give their patients meat to eat might as well be handing out free cigarettes. It would make as much sense, do less harm to the environment and probably be cheaper.

Not that it is just the meat in the hospital diet that causes problems. The quality of the food served to patients in our hospitals is beyond appalling. You are more likely to contract a food bug in an NHS hospital than just about anywhere else in Britain. What an awful thing it is that NHS hospital food is more likely to make you ill than a hot dog bought from a street vendor's stall.

The way the food is served is a scandal too.

The cleaners put down their mops and hand out the food. Naturally, they don't bother to wash their hands. If the patient is physically incapable of eating what's been put before them then the tray is simply taken away.

'We're not allowed to feed patients,' one cleaner told me.

'I'm here to nurse,' one overweight nurse told me. 'I'm not here to feed patients.' I had a suspicion that she was eating up all the leftovers.

It is common for patients who are not visited by relatives to starve to death in hospital.

The bottom line is that the food in most NHS hospitals is at best inedible and at worst dangerous. There is rarely enough of it. It is often badly chosen and badly prepared. Patients of all types desperately need good food if they are to have the best chance of recovering. But food-related illnesses are commonplace in hospitals. And nurses are so lazy and disinterested that thousands of patients starve to death because they cannot reach the food that is put in front of them. Just about every dietician, nutritionist and cook working for the NHS should be charged with multiple manslaughter.

When my mother had breast cancer she wisely stopped eating meat and adopted a vegetarian diet. She did not take the tamoxifen tablets the consultant oncologist prescribed. And she refused the radiotherapy they recommended. She beat the cancer with diet.

When she was admitted to hospital with her final illness, the staff were told that she was vegetarian. They took no notice. In both Exeter and Budleigh hospitals, the staff persisted in offering her meat-based dishes. When my mother was given a meal of sausages, I complained to one of the nurses. I explained that my mother was vegetarian. The nurse told me that my mother could have a Cornish pasty instead of the sausage.

On another occasion, early in her final illness, I was sitting beside my mother's bed when she was brought a meal consisting of cottage pie and boiled potatoes. Her menu slip had been filled in by someone else because she was too confused to do it herself. 'This is cottage pie,' I said to my mother. 'Do you want it?' She thought for a long time. She was becoming demented because of the normal pressure hydrocephalus the doctors refused to accept was causing her symptoms, but knew that there was something wrong. It was clearly a great effort for her. 'I don't eat cottage pie,' she replied at last. 'Why not?' I asked her quietly. 'It's not the sort of thing I eat,' she replied at last. 'I don't eat meat.'

When we did finally persuade the hospital staff to provide vegetarian food, they provided very little variety. When I was feeding her pieces of an insipid looking cheese and leek flan she said, with great heart-felt weariness: 'I've had a lot of that.'

The Government, whose advisers know of the relationship between meat consumption and cancer, spends taxpayers' money on promoting the sale and consumption of meat.

Thomas Jefferson was perfectly correct when he wrote: 'If people let Government decide what foods they eat, and what medicines they take, their bodies will soon be in as sorry a state as are the souls of those who live under tyranny.'

And despite the fact that people who eat lots of burgers are more likely to develop cancer than people who eat a healthier diet ('Eat McCrap, develop McCancer and McDie' might not be a catchy slogan but I offer it without charge), Britain's Department of Health has invited McDonald's, (and other processed food companies) to help write Government policy on obesity and diet related diseases.

# G

## GERIATRICIANS

Too many geriatricians have little interest in patients, let alone old people. Geriatrics is an unfashionable speciality, unpopular with doctors because it's not glamorous and offers little opportunity for the big fees to be earned from private practice. Geriatrics is so unpopular among doctors that it is the speciality chosen by doctors who want to become consultants as quickly as possible.

## GOVERNMENT

Your government wants you dead. Screw 'em: stay alive as long as possible. And piss off the moody, miserable, selfish politicians by letting them see you are enjoying life.

# H

## HEARING

Hearing starts to deteriorate at the age of about 30 and begins with the loss of high-pitched sounds.

If your hearing has deteriorated to the point where you need a hearing aid, see your doctor and ask for a referral. Never, ever buy a hearing aid from a company which advertises in magazines, has a chain of high street shops, shoves a leaflet through your letterbox or, worst of all, sends someone round to knock on your door and offer you a free hearing test. Everyone associated with such companies is a cheat, a crook and a trickster and if you live high enough up in a block of flats, just kick them down the stairs.

Remember that much deafness can be cured in five minutes by having your ears syringed and the wax removed.

## HIGH BLOOD PRESSURE

On 22nd February 2011, the British Government warned that a large number of patients who were being treated for high blood pressure didn't actually have high blood pressure.

How this could possibly be described as news is quite beyond me.

I first warned that blood pressure was being over treated over 30 years ago.

Naturally, I was pilloried for it by the medical establishment and the medical press.

But it wasn't a difficult conclusion to draw.

As a GP, I often acquired new patients who had been given repeat prescriptions for powerful anti-hypertensive therapies for years without ever seeing a doctor.

In the early 1970s, I was criticised viciously for daring to suggest that blood pressure could often be raised by stress and could, therefore, be brought under control if sufferers learned how to control their stress.

Moreover, it is often remarkably easy for people with moderately high blood pressure to bring their blood pressure down simply by making moderate lifestyle changes (losing weight, giving up cigarettes, taking gentle exercise, reducing their exposure to stress and so on.)

I have lost count of the number of readers who have followed my advice on this and been able to bring their blood pressure under control – often to the astonishment of their own doctors.

Why does it always take doctors so long to see the obvious?

The answer, of course, is that doctors are controlled by drug companies. And drug companies prefer to treat every symptom or sign with drugs – whether it is necessary to do so or not.

Today, more than 8.5 million people in the UK are registered as having high blood pressure. All are treated with expensive and dangerous drugs. The Government now says that a quarter of these don't have it. That is a massive under-estimate. At least a half of them do not have high blood pressure – and never had it.

And, at least half of the remaining half could control their blood pressure without drug treatment.

## HOLISTIC MEDICINE

Holistic medicine means treating the patient in whatever way will produce effective, safe results. It means combining orthodox and alternative medicine.

The word 'holistic' was first introduced in 1926 by the South African philosopher and statesman Jan Christian Smuts. He suggested that the whole human being is much more than (and quite different to) a collection of physical or emotional parts. Back in those dark days there were doctors parading up and down hospital wards referring to the 'liver' in the end bed and the 'case of pancreatitis' in the third bed on the left. What am I talking about? There still are.

But whatever they may claim there are virtually no 'holistic' hospitals around. And there are no holistic healers. If you want holistic medicine then you must become a holistic patient. The problem is that an intuitive, holistic approach goes against everything with which the bureaucratic, legalistic, constrained medical establishment feels comfortable. The medical establishment was bought by the drug industry decades ago. Modern medicine is geared to solving problems with drugs, surgery or radiotherapy and does not acknowledge the influence of stress or diet. Nor does the medical establishment appreciate the importance of preventive medicine.

The myth that drug therapy offers the only true solution is now repeated unquestioningly and without hesitation or embarrassment. Many members of the medical establishment believe that medical advances largely depend upon the pharmaceutical industry. This is not regarded as a subject for debate but as a fundamental building block; a fact of medical life.

It is not surprising, therefore, that the drug company owned and controlled medical establishment still looks with horror at all varieties of alternative medicine. Attempts to organise research programmes into the effectiveness of acupuncture, herbalism or homoeopathy are invariably treated with a sneer or a patronising dismissal.

It is one of the great scandals of the 21st century that the billion dollar worldwide cancer industry, the international drug industry and the medical 'profession' (now, more of a trade than a 'profession') would all much rather suppress an alternative cancer treatment rather than have to admit that orthodox remedies might be bettered.

Doctors pay lip service to holistic medicine but what they really mean is that patients should be prepared to try a wide variety of drugs and orthodox medical treatments. Hospital specialists have drifted into intellectual parochialism. Most now specialise and then specialise again. They are absurdly narrow-minded and bigoted; there is no integration, no overview and no common sense.

'Holistic' (or, as it sometimes spelt, wholistic) medicine has, for several decades, been growing in theoretical popularity. Many alternative and some orthodox health care professionals describe themselves as 'holistic' practitioners. But most aren't. Most journalists inaccurately assume that the word is a synonym for 'alternative' or 'complementary' medicine. But that is wrong too.

The word and the concept lay more or less forgotten until the 1970s when the growth of high technology medicine led to a revolution among patients who felt that aggressive, interventionist medicine wasn't entirely satisfactory.

Suddenly there was a widespread, sensible feeling that specialisation and fragmentation were not all they had been cracked up to be.

In practical terms the use of the word 'holistic' meant, in theory at least, that instead of regarding patients as sick kidneys or hearts, health care professionals would try to meet the physical, mental, emotional and spiritual needs of their patients by dealing with social problems as well as physical ones and by using natural healing methods as well as modern, pharmacological or surgical techniques.

In short, the word 'holistic' was intended to describe an attitude. An attitude which can be just as well followed by an orthodox trained doctor as by an alternative practitioner. A general practitioner in a busy city health centre can be 'holistic' in his approach just as easily as can a herbalist or acupuncturist working from a back bedroom.

There is no doubt that a truly 'holistic' approach to medical care is extremely good news for patients.

When followed properly it means that every illness can be treated with a 'pick and mix' approach – choosing whichever aspects of orthodox and alternative medicine are most likely to be effective, and least likely to produce side effects, and treating and taking full notice of all aspects of the individual's being.

It is a fact that in most illnesses there is no point in treating what is wrong with the body unless you also treat what is wrong with the mind and it seems to me remarkable that a modern doctor will treat the body of a patient who is suffering from high blood pressure, irritable bowel syndrome or asthma but ignore the mind, when it is now established beyond doubt that in so many illnesses the physical symptoms are produced by mental turmoil of one sort or another.

It is equally bizarre and, in truth, unscientific, for an osteopath to treat a patient's back and ignore his mind.

The advantages of a truly 'holistic' approach are colossal not only because 'holistic' medicine offers a chance to use the best and avoid the worst but also because different types of treatment can, when used together, have a synergistic effect. A genuinely 'holistic' approach may use a modern drug, a relaxation technique and a type of massage to tackle a single collection of symptoms.

But although in theory the word 'holistic' implies an admirable change in attitude there is, sadly, little evidence that practitioners really understand what the word means or how it should be applied in practice.

It would be nice to think that everyone could find a 'holistic' practitioner to look after them. But don't hold your breath. You've about as much chance of striking oil when digging in your winter vegetables.

The bottom line is that I don't think that many patients are ever going to receive truly 'holistic' treatment from their practitioners. Most training programmes are, by their very nature, designed to produce specialists. Medical schools turn out drug dispensers and cutters. And there aren't many health care professionals with the time or inclination to study other available specialities.

We must also recognise that there is, of course, a huge financial disincentive involved here. How many practitioners are going to suggest to a paying patient that he would obtain better treatment by visiting another professional?

All this is enormously depressing.

But it doesn't mean that 'holistic' medicine is out of reach. What it does mean is that if you really want 'holistic' treatment (and in my opinion you should) you're going to have to take control yourself if you or anyone in your family needs treatment.

Devise your own 'pick and mix' approach.

It really is the only sensible way.


## HOSPITALS

Hospitals are terrible places. People die in them. You should go into hospital only as a last resort. And you should escape the minute you can. As a doctor I am ashamed, saddened and embarrassed to have to tell you this but hospital patients are routinely neglected, humiliated and left in pain. Thousands of patients have died as a result of poor treatment. One independent enquiry documented cases where patients had been left unwashed for up to a month and left without food, drink and medical treatment. The conclusion was that managers had been 'preoccupied with cost-cutting, targets and processes' and had lost sight of their basic responsibilities. Astonishingly, none of the responsible managers responsible was taken to court. Nor were any of the doctors and nurses punished.

I have little doubt that in all the hospitals where patients have been dying unnecessarily the staff (including doctors and nurses) managed to convince themselves that they were providing patients with excellent service.

And, equally, I have no doubt that an enormous number of patients and relatives and hospital visitors must have ignored all these awful things and believed that the hospitals concerned were doing a wonderful job.

It wouldn't surprise me in the slightest to hear that the managers responsible for all this pain, agony and death, have thick files of letters from patients and relatives thanking them for the excellent care.

The truth is that neither patients nor relatives know precisely what to expect from hospitals.

Walk into an NHS hospital and you will find demented patients in awful pain. You will find patients with terrible bedsores (the bedsore is a classic sign of bad nursing). You will find patients who are starving to death or dying of dehydration because the staff can't be bothered to feed them or give them fluids. You will see patients so dehydrated that their lips are bleeding and sore and, when gently pinched, their dried out skin stays where you've put it. You will see patients dumped in a chair, sitting in urine soaked incontinence pads which have clearly not been changed for hours. You will see obvious signs of malnutrition. These aren't patients in Third World countries. They aren't patients in badly run care homes. They are patients in major NHS hospitals. I know it is true because I have seen it time and time again with my eyes.

Patients awaiting surgery are sent home because the hospital has run out of money and can't afford the sutures and other surgical equipment needed to operate on them. An 83-year-old woman with dementia was sent home from hospital in the middle of the night without her family being informed. The next day she was found dead, alone in her bedroom.

Dirty sheets are reused in hospitals, just as they are in the dirtiest, cheapest, nastiest doss houses. But hospitals aren't supposed to be doss houses. They are places where the people in the beds are, by definition, all ill. Many of them with infectious diseases. I can understand bureaucrats accepting the re-use of dirty sheets. They are nasty, uncaring people. But doctors and nurses?

Dignity and respect are not words which the modern hospital employee understands. Not, at least, when applied to patients. Many hospitals still have mixed wards – with male and female patients forced to abandon their natural dignity in the interests of hospital economy (so that the administrators can take yet another huge pay rise). Governments repeatedly promise to make sure that mixed wards are done away with. Inevitably, this promise is quickly forgotten and abandoned.

A generation or so ago most hospitals employed an almoner. It was her job (and the job was invariably held by a woman) to take care of patients' social problems. If an elderly patient was worried about the cat she'd left at home the almoner would find someone to feed it. If a patient was going home after a long stay in hospital the almoner would help ensure that the house was prepared. The almoner played a vital part in helping patients rest and recover.

Today, none of these things is done.

And yet our hospitals are awash with social workers who regard practical problems as beneath them and spend their days organising meetings to discuss meetings.

The result of all this is that NHS hospitals are best at dealing with mechanical, easy solvable, easily identifiable problems. If you have an uncomplicated broken leg then a hospital will probably be able to deal with it efficiently and relatively safely – as long as you manage to convalesce at home rather than on a hospital ward. With other, more complicated problems, however, hospitals can do a great deal more harm than good.

Back in the Middle Ages people were terrified to go into hospital. They knew it was a sentence of death. Relatives started digging your grave as you went through the doors of the local infirmary. Things are getting that way again.

British hospitals are now among the worst in the world. One survey of NHS staff showed that only 44% thought that they would be happy with the standard of care provided if they were patients in their own hospital. Many British patients are now travelling half way round the world to get treatment in hospitals where patients are treated quickly, efficiently, hygienically and with respect. So, for example, hospitals in India are offering attractive package deals for British patients who can't wait two years for treatment or who don't fancy the idea of being killed by an antibiotic-resistant hospital infection. Officially, adverse drug reactions kill 18,000 people a year and cause 600,000 hospital admissions in the UK every year. In reality, things are far, far worse than that.

And although it is called a National Health Service, it isn't. In 1971, I made a television programme for the BBC in which I explained that there were massive variations in the types of treatment available in different parts of the country. I used a blackboard, a long stick, a large map and several large sheets of paper to explain how treatments varied in different parts of the country. (This was, of course, long before the days of computer graphics.) There was, I claimed, no real 'national' health service. Nothing has changed in principle although I suppose it is quite likely that there have been changes in the nature of the inequalities prevalent in the various regions. To call it a 'National' Health Service is an absurdity that should merit investigation.

One of the common arguments in favour of the NHS is that everyone gets the treatment they need without having to pay for it. This is, of course, a myth. Even allowing for the fact that some patients are denied treatment on the grounds of cost, and others are denied treatment simply because the area where they live does not offer the treatment they need, there is another big problem: NHS staff select patients for treatment on the basis of their perceived need and 'value' to society.

Some readers may be shocked to know that the National Health Service already operates a selection system for treatment.

But it has done so for many years. (English patients are particularly likely to be affected. Scottish hospitals have plenty of money; though it comes, of course, from English taxpayers.)

When treatment is expensive, it is provided for those patients who are regarded as the most deserving. And how does our system decide which patients are most deserving? Simple. A young married man with lots of children will be at the top of the list. An elderly man who lives alone will be right at the bottom of the list.

And so the NHS will provide life-saving treatment for an unemployed scrounger of 36 who has a wife, a mistress and eight children. But a great, elderly painter or composer will be allowed to die.

Nurses, not doctors, decide whether or not patients should die. It is nurses who decide whether or not patients should be resuscitated.

Meanwhile, as people die for a lack of resources, the NHS merrily spends millions on hiring translators for patients who cannot speak English. The NHS provides translators for 160 languages including Cherokee and Cebuano. The fact that there are no registered users of those languages in Britain doesn't seem to concern the people with the cheque books. (Try visiting a hospital in Turkey or Greece and asking for a free translator.)

And is it not absurd, unfair and just plain wrong that NHS money is spent on providing couples with fertility treatment and women with breast enlargement operations while thousands of patients are dying because they have to wait weeks for essential, simple diagnostic X-rays?

Surely, life-saving should come first and life enhancing come second?

In military hospital units, doctors operate a simple but effective system whereby those whose need is greatest get seen first. It's a sound principle. Life-saving should come first and life enhancing should come second.

But in the NHS the people who receive the best (and fastest) treatment are the patients who are represented by the most efficient lobbyists. The elderly, needless to say, have no one fighting in their corner. And so people wanting cosmetic surgery, sex change surgery, infertility treatment and other lifestyle medicine have their needs met while the elderly are denied basic treatment which would in some cases transform their lives and others save their lives.

Today, well over twice as many people are killed in hospitals by infections as are killed on the roads.

The reason? Filthy wards, unhygienic practices, scandalously poor cleaning, grubby operating theatres and staff who never wash their hands. There are more such infections in British hospitals than anywhere else in the world. Why? Simple. British hospitals are dirtier than hospitals anywhere else in the world. Why? The staff in British hospitals are the laziest and most incompetent hospital staff in the world.

If you live in Britain and have to go to hospital for any operation or procedure, you now have a 50% chance of getting a worse disease from being in the hospital. That's official. And if you do survive the experience and get to go home there is a good chance that you will leave malnourished. Staggeringly, one in five National Health Service (NHS) patients leaves hospital officially malnourished. Some patients don't eat because the food is inedible and looks unappetising. For others the taste and quality of the food is irrelevant; they stay hungry because no one helps them eat it. Staff dump food on a patient's table and then collect it, untouched, half an hour later. The patient, starving hungry, hasn't eaten because he or she was too weak to reach the food. Staff put food in front of semi-conscious patients and then walk away. In the 21st century, NHS the patients slowly starve to death. One NHS patient who was blind couldn't see the food put before her. No one bothered to feed her.

Other patients complain that the food they are given is shrink wrapped in impenetrable plastic. It's a sort of modern NHS torture. The patient can see the food but they can't get at it.

NHS hospitals are now so badly run, so filthy, so unprofessionally managed that they are likely to do more harm than good.

The evidence has shown for years that many patients who have heart attacks are better off staying at home than going into hospital.

Hospitals have become unsuitable for the healthy – let alone the sick.

In general, patients will survive for longer if they avoid the NHS. The survival rates in NHS institutions are awful. The standard of health care is among the worst in the world. Hospitals are run by people who don't give a damn about anything other than bonuses.

Whether you are at home or in hospital it is, at night and weekends, easier to find a plumber prepared to come out than it is to find a doctor prepared to visit.

An NHS manager in charge of the complaints system in a London hospital fell ill and needed treatment as an in-patient. He afterwards admitted that he 'got into difficulties finding out who was his doctor, what medicine to take and when he was getting out'.

What a bloody country. What a bloody NHS. What a bloody disgrace.

People in Britain pay to go into private hospitals not because they expect to be treated more kindly, or because they expect better medical treatment, but because they hope that they will not be allowed to die from starvation or thirst and they believe, probably correctly, that the wards will be cleaner.

It is, perhaps, hardly surprising that the people who run (and work for) the National Health Service, prefer not to use it. Civil servants working at the Department of Health are entitled to be members of the Benendeen Healthcare Society which serves one million British Telecom, Post office and civil service workers. If they fall ill, they get to go to a luxury private hospital. Staff at the General Medical Council are provided free membership of a private health care company.

A third of Britain's general practitioners (GPs) would prefer private treatment for themselves and their families. Hospital consultants are the same. Here's what one NHS consultant had to say: 'In the past we knew we would get good care on the NHS. I don't trust it any more. Even I can't bully my way through the system.'

An increasing number of hospital doctors now buy private health care insurance so that they and their families won't have to endure NHS care. Trade unions defend the NHS and oppose any reforms but many of them have done deals with private sector organisations to provide private health care insurance so that their members don't have to use the NHS. More than half of the TUC's members have some sort of private medical insurance. This is a higher proportion than any other socio-economic group in the UK.

Most people working in the NHS admit that if they (or a member of their family) fall ill they would not want to be treated in the hospital where they work. I will repeat that. Most people working in the NHS admit that if they (or a member of their family) fall ill they would not want to be treated in the hospital where they work.

(The NHS used to ask staff members if they'd be happy to be treated in their hospital. It was part of their public relations propaganda. After they found that just one in four members of staff would recommend the hospital where they worked to relatives or friends, or be happy to use it themselves, the question was quietly dropped. Would you take your car to a garage knowing that three out of four mechanics who worked there wouldn't trust the garage with their own car?)

Tables which rank British hospitals invariably show that independent hospitals do much better than NHS hospitals in every measurable respect. Patients are treated better and they get better quicker. It is, perhaps, hardly surprising that just about every patient in the country (and every sane one) would, if given a choice, choose to have an operation in a private hospital rather than an NHS hospital.

Politicians claim that they think the NHS is wonderful. They say that they wouldn't dream of going into a private hospital. But they don't have to wait to see a doctor and if they need in-patient treatment they go into private rooms where they are waited on hand and foot. They get private care without it costing them a penny.

Hospitals are obsessed with curing (which they aren't terribly good at) and don't understand, or have time for, the principles of caring. For example, many hospitals refuse to allow visitors to take flowers into hospitals – arguing that flowers are a nuisance. This is sad. It has been known for thousands of years that patients are far more likely to get better quickly in hospitals which are bright, light, airy and filled with gentle music and fresh flowers. Since the first hospitals were built it has been recognised that the colour and perfume which flowers add to hospitals contribute greatly to the rate at which patients recover. Good hospitals are peaceful and are designed around a courtyard so that convalescent patients can walk in the cloisters and look at the flowers. But modern hospitals are designed for the convenience of the administrators. Patients are a bloody nuisance. I have recently been in several hospitals where the floors were carpeted because this made it nicer for the administrators when they were going to meetings. Naturally, the floors were stained with blood, urine and all the other remnants which would normally be wiped up off the floor. You can't ever properly clean a carpeted floor in a busy hospital because if the corridor is closed for proper cleaning the wards will be cut off. I know hospitals where the car park nearest the hospital entrance is reserved for administrators.

Patients – however sick or frail they may be – have to walk, shuffle or limp half a mile, possibly in the rain.

And why do hospitals clamp the cars of patients and visitors?

Do they really think people want to spend more time than necessary in these places?

One large hospital, which is not atypical, has 6,000 members of staff and 1,800 spaces for their cars. The inevitable result is that doctors, nurses and cleaners have to park in the spaces allocated for patients and relatives who, therefore, cannot find anywhere to park at all. Patients whose appointments are delayed find themselves having to pay extortionate fines.

Time and time again I have received letters from readers telling me that while having tests (and waiting to be seen at yet another department) they had, on top of all their other worries, been frightened that they would outstay the maximum three hour waiting period and would return to their vehicle to find it clamped.

I know of a hospital where the architect and bureaucrats put the psychiatric ward on the 6th floor. The ward had fully opening windows and a concrete walkway underneath. To everyone's astonishment, the ward has a much higher rate of successful suicides than other comparable hospital psychiatric wards. The incidence of attempted suicides was no higher. But, despite a good many meetings, the administrators couldn't work out why the success rate among suicides was so high.

The vast majority of patients hand over their health (and their lives) to their doctors – without ever questioning what is happening to them. That is a dangerous way to live. Patients who take an interest in their own health may sometimes feel that the doctors and nurses who are looking after them regard them as a nuisance. But all the evidence shows clearly that such patients get better quicker, suffer fewer unpleasant side effects and live longer than patients who simply lie back passively and allow the professionals to take over. If your doctor wants you to take a drug make sure you know what to expect. If your doctor wants you to have surgery then make sure that you know what the surgery entails, what the possible consequences might be and what the alternatives are. Good questions to ask are: 'Would you have this operation if you were me?' or: 'Would you recommend this operation to someone in your close family?'

Hospitals are so bad that it is, perhaps, hardly surprising that I have for some years now recommended that every patient going into hospital should take a supply of disinfectant wipes, a mobile telephone, the telephone number of a local 24 hour taxi service (in case they want to escape) and the phone numbers of at least three newspapers.

Remember: GPs kill retail but hospitals kill wholesale.

## HOUSE CALLS (HOME VISITS)

Half a century ago, it was commonplace for doctors to make house calls to their older patients on a regular basis. Believe it or not, doctors would actually call on elderly patients even when they hadn't been asked to do so.

Back in those old days, GPs were invariably ready to visit patients at home if requested to do so.

In the United Kingdom, GPs who made house calls were the basis of the NHS.

Sadly, this service has been all but destroyed by three forces. The General Medical Council forced older GPs to retire. A recent Labour Government gave doctors the option to stop providing 24 hour cover. And EU laws about working hours forced doctors to adopt the sort of working hours previously enjoyed by librarians and planning officials.

My advice to all older patients is, first and foremost, try to register with a doctor who is prepared to visit his patients at home. If you can find a doctor who does his own calls at night and at weekends clutch him tightly to your bosom for he is a rare as a mare's nest.

## HYGIENE

A few decades ago, in a book called *Superbody*, I warned that infections were about to make a big return to our lives. Many people (including doctors and nurses) felt certain that medicine had pretty well conquered most common, lethal bugs.

I didn't. I felt that the overprescribing of antibiotics was bound to result in the bugs acquiring immunity.

And I'm afraid I was right. The bugs we thought we'd conquered are back big time. And poor hygiene practices in hospitals have given us a whole new range of super-infections.

As a result, most popular antibiotics are now often ineffective. It was an entirely predictable problem but it is too late to moan now about opportunities missed and warnings ignored.

The plain fact is that many killer bugs have become immune to antibiotics.

And things are, I'm afraid, going to get worse.

The result is that bugs are now a major cause of death – particularly among the frail, the sick and the elderly. Vast numbers of old people die of chest infections.

Of course, doctors tell people that they can prevent infections with their damned vaccines. But I'm afraid this is rubbish. Like all vaccines, the one which is given to protect against the flu does more harm than good. (I know this is an unpopular point of view but I don't really care anymore. I've issued more accurate warnings and predictions than any other doctor and I'm sticking with this one.)

There are two good ways to reduce your risk of catching a lethal infection and neither of them involves drugs or vaccines.

First, try to keep your immune system in tip top shape. Your body's immune system protects you against all sorts of diseases, including infections and cancer, and it isn't difficult to keep it in good working order. Just make sure that you eat plenty of foods such as fresh fruit and vegetables that contain vitamins.

Second, avoid catching other people's infections by taking great care not to pick up their bugs. This is especially important advice if you live in a hospital, hotel or residential home of any kind. The chances are, I'm afraid, that the nurses will consider themselves above cleaning and the cleaners won't have been taught how easily bugs can be spread. Keep antiseptic wipes with you at all times and use them to clean taps, door handles, lavatory seats and handles and everything else you have to touch. Make sure that crockery and cutlery are clean before you use them. Ignore anyone who sneers and says you're a nutter. You'll have the last laugh because they'll be dead.

# HYPOTHERMIA

Every year tens of thousands of old people die of the cold; they die because they can't afford to keep warm. The average winter kills around 60,000 old people. A bad winter kills far more.

This suits the politicians. It means that there are fewer old people around claiming pensions.

Gas and electricity companies aren't supposed to cut off supplies to the frail elderly and impoverished. So they put in a meter and refuse to supply gas or electricity until the bills are paid.

Every winter, politicians and charities tell old people to move their bed and all their belongings into one room so that they only have one room to heat.

Have you ever heard such patronising rubbish?

I wonder how many of the people giving this absurd advice actually try living in one room dominated by a bed?

British taxpayers still pay out £1,000,000 a year each to over 1,000 bankers at the bankrupt bank Royal Bank of Scotland where arrogance seems to be a substitute for intelligence. Fred Goodwin, the boss whose methods resulted in that bank's collapse, receives a pension of the best part of £1,000,000 a year. UK banks have had to pay out £75 billion in fines, compensation and legal costs as a result of crooked and dishonest practices and yet the hubristic psychopaths responsible have been rewarded not with lengthy prison sentences but with massive payoffs and pensions that make lottery winnings look mean.

If a fraction of that money had been handed out to vulnerable pensioners no one would die of the cold in the winter.

# I

## IATROGENESIS

This is not a word you will hear doctors using very often. It means an illness which has been caused by a medical examination or treatment.

Iatrogenic disease is disease caused by doctors.

The modern medical profession has become very dangerous and iatrogenesis (illness or death caused by doctors) is now one of the top three killers – alongside cancer and circulatory disease.

The result is that the person most likely to kill you is not a mugger, not a burglar, not a drunken driver and not an enraged relative. It is your doctor.

Modern, Western doctors, equipped with fancy drugs, exotic forms of surgery and impressive sounding radiotherapy techniques, are ranked alongside cancer, heart disease and stroke as major killers.

Four out of ten patients who are given drugs suffer serious and sometimes potentially lethal side effects. If the drug you're prescribed is going to save your life that's probably an acceptable risk. But how many patients who are merely suffering from something annoying or uncomfortable would willingly take a drug if they knew it might kill them? There are hugely profitable drugs on the market which have never saved any lives but which have killed or made ill countless thousands of people.

One in six patients in hospital is there only because he has been made ill by doctors. Most are suffering from unpleasant or downright dangerous drug side effects. In America, bad reactions to legal drugs kill far more people annually than all illegal drug use combined.

You won't hear any of this from most doctors, of course. Doctors are notoriously reluctant to admit that the treatments they recommend can do harm. There are several reasons for this.

First, they often don't know how dangerous drugs and other treatments can be. In just about every Westernised country in the world, doctors receive most of their post graduate education through meetings and journals which are sponsored by drug companies. And drug companies don't spend too much of their time warning doctors about drug side effects. Global drug companies don't exist to find cures or help people: they exist solely to make money.

Second, doctors are frightened of being sued.

Third, there are nearly half a million clinical research papers published every week. No doctor on the planet can read them all – or even have the faintest idea what warnings they might give. Useful reports are lost among the irrelevant, commercially inspired dross. Any evidence showing that doctors and drug companies are killing people is easily overlooked or allowed to slip behind a convenient filing cabinet.

Finally, the natural human unwillingness to admit responsibility is exceptionally well developed among doctors who often think of themselves as having god-like qualities. Admitting to mistakes reminds doctors that they are human and fallible.

The bottom line is that during the last century, doctors and drug companies have become louder, more aggressive, a good deal richer and far more powerful but life expectancy has not risen as a result of any of their activities.

## ILLNESS

Illness is rarer among old people than young.

Over 65s tend to have 1.3 illnesses per year each on average.

Under 65s tend to have 2.1 illnesses per year each on average.

The figures prove that illness isn't the same thing as ageing, it can occur at any age.

Diseases tend to affect us more slowly when we are old. As a result, many 90-year-olds have at least half a dozen serious health problems – often causing very little trouble.

Men often have prostate cancer which has been trundling along harmlessly for years. I suspect more elderly men die or suffer because their prostate cancer has been aggressively and unnecessarily diagnosed and treated than die because of prostate cancer itself.

# INFECTIONS

A few decades ago, the development of antibiotics led many people to believe that the threat offered by infectious diseases had, to a large extent, been conquered.

But a combination of greed and stupidity has changed all that.

The effectiveness of antibiotics has been dramatically weakened by three main groups: the companies making them, the medical profession and the farming industry. Each of these groups has acted irresponsibly and dangerously. Since they cannot possibly have been unaware of the impact their actions would have, it is impossible to avoid the conclusion that the effectiveness of antibiotics has been deliberately destroyed for short-term profit.

The drug companies, the medical establishment and the farming industry will together be responsible for millions of deaths around the world. The politicians who have stood to one side and allowed all this to happen must share the responsibility.

During the last few decades simple, widespread infections have been striking back and re-establishing themselves as serious threats to our health. Today, our hospitals are dangerous places for the healthy – and far too dangerous for the sick.

In 1952, virtually all infections caused by staphylococcus could be cured by penicillin. But just 30 years later, a worrying 90% of patients infected with the staphylococcus bug needed treatment with other antibiotics. Western doctors didn't worry about this because they had other antibiotics to prescribe. With remarkable arrogance, the medical profession in America and Europe assumed that it could always stay one step ahead of the bugs. What many doctors failed to realise was that yeasts, fungi and bacteria have been producing antibiotics more or less since time began. They use the antibiotics they make to protect themselves. Other yeasts, fungi and bacteria mutate naturally in order to protect themselves against those antibiotics. Through a mixture of ignorance and arrogance doctors speeded up the rate at which bugs acquired resistance, by spreading antibiotics around with reckless abandon. Overwhelmed by reckless enthusiasm, doctors started routinely giving antibiotics to all the patients whom they thought might be at risk – and this category often included all those patients who were destined for surgery. The prescribing doctors either didn't realise or didn't care that by dishing out antibiotics so freely they were giving the bacteria a greatly increased chance of acquiring immunity.

Staphylococcus has not, of course, been the only bug to become resistant and the Western medical establishment, constantly afraid of offending the drug companies, has done everything possible to stifle protests and warnings about the consequences. Today the future is truly bleak. Infectious diseases which we thought we had conquered are coming back with a vengeance. More and more people are dying of simple, uncomplicated infections. The bugs are getting stronger. And our ability to kill them is diminishing almost daily.

Today, one in six prescriptions is for an antibiotic and my educated guestimate is that between 50% and 90% of all these prescriptions are unnecessary or inappropriate. To a certain extent doctors over-prescribe because they like to do something when faced with a patient – and prescribing a drug is virtually the only thing most of them can do. And to some extent prescribing a drug is a defence against any possible future charge of negligence (on the basis that if the patient dies it is better to have done something than to have done nothing). But the main reason for the over-prescribing of antibiotics is, without doubt, the fact that doctors are under the influence of the drug companies. The makers of the antibiotics want their drugs prescribed in vast quantities. It makes no difference to them whether or not the prescriptions are necessary.

Things are made worse by the fact that although antibiotics have been around for over half a century, and the drug companies making them must have made billions of dollars in profits, no one yet knows how long antibiotic tablets should really be taken for when treating any specific condition. Should you take an antibiotic course for 5, 7, 10 or 14 days? The bizarre truth is that your guess is probably as good as your doctor's and his is probably as good as the drug company's.

The over-prescribing of antibiotics would not matter too much if these drugs were harmless and if there were no other hazards associated with their use. But antibiotics are certainly not harmless. The unnecessary and excessive use of antibiotics causes allergy reactions, side effects and a huge variety of serious complications – including the ultimate complication: death. And, of course, there is also the very real hazard that by overusing antibiotics, doctors are enabling bacteria to develop immunity to these potentially life-saving drugs. There is now no doubt that many of our most useful drugs have been devalued by overuse and are no longer effective. The overprescribing of antibiotics is extraordinarily dangerous and constantly underestimated. It is far more of a threat to human life, and more of a threat to our future, than terrorism. The unnecessary antibiotics we have swallowed by the ton have weakened our general resistance to infection and paradoxically, strengthened the power of the bugs.

The existence of many antibiotic-resistant organisms is the main reason why infections are such a major problem in hospitals. Alarmingly, at least 1 in 20 of all hospital patients will pick up an infection in hospital – mostly urinary tract, chest or wound infections. The spread of these antibiotic-resistant organisms is mostly caused by doctors and nurses failing to wash their hands often enough. The problem is so great that the extra costs incurred when doctors have to prescribe increasingly expensive antibiotics are beginning to add an enormous burden to all those responsible for providing health care facilities. In America, the extra cost of dealing with antibiotic-resistant organisms is many billions of dollars a year.

Partly thanks to doctors and drug companies, the future is truly bleak. Infectious diseases which we thought we had conquered are coming back with a vengeance. More and more people are dying of simple, uncomplicated infections. The bugs are getting stronger. And our ability to kill them is diminishing almost daily.

However, the problem isn't entirely the result of overprescribing by doctors. The overuse of antibiotics by farmers is another big reason why infectious diseases are making a dramatic comeback. Astonishingly, considerably more than half of all the antibiotics sold are given by farmers to healthy animals.

Farmers claim that their animals are only given antibiotics when they have been recommended by a vet. Of course this is true. Farmers cannot buy antibiotics without a vet. But sadly, there are enough money hungry vets around to make sure that any farmer who wants to give his animals continuous doses of antibiotics will have no supply problem. I talked to one vet who regularly prescribed huge quantities of antibiotics for farmers to give to healthy cattle.

'Don't you realise that what you are doing is endangering the lives of millions of human beings?' I asked him. He shrugged; he clearly knew I was right but clearly didn't care. 'Why do you do it?' I asked him. 'The farmers demand them,' he said with blunt honesty. 'If I don't prescribe antibiotics someone else will and I'll lose the farm business.'

Why do farmers give their animals so many antibiotics?

Well, some, of course, are prescribed to help prevent (and treat) disease. Animals on modern western farms are exceptionally susceptible to disease because they are kept in overcrowded conditions and they are constantly highly stressed. Antibiotics help to keep sick animals alive long enough to be slaughtered and fed into the food chain. Antibiotics are also given because they help to stop diseases spreading quickly among animals who are kept in cramped and entirely unnatural conditions. When animals live in hideously confined quarters it is nigh on impossible to stop infections spreading without using antibiotics. Many American and European farmers routinely put antibiotics into the feed they give their animals to prevent infections developing. The antibiotics that are dished out in this grossly irresponsible way are often the same antibiotics that are becoming dramatically less effective in the treatment of human diseases.

But farmers don't just give antibiotics to animals in order to deal with disease. They also put antibiotics into their animal feed in order to promote growth. Antibiotics increase the muscle bulk of animals – and therefore increase their value and the farmer's eventual profit.

The process by which antibiotic resistance develops on farms is simple to explain. When animals are given antibiotics, the bacteria in their intestines build up an immunity to those antibiotics. Those antibiotic-resistant organisms then pass on to farmers and others who have contact with the animals. They pass into the environment (even though most animals are denied access to fields, their faeces and urine still reach the environment when they are dumped onto fields or discharged into rivers). And, of course, the antibiotic-resistant organisms pass into the food chain directly when animals are killed, chopped up and eaten by humans. When milk in the USA was tested, researchers identified 52 different antibiotic residues.

Between them, doctors and farmers have put us all at risk. Around the world, millions of innocent people will die because bugs have now acquired immunity to previously valuable antibiotics.

The problem is exacerbated because our hospitals are filthy and the people who staff them probably can't even spell hygiene. Having talked to many doctors and nurses, I am convinced that most don't know the basic principles of how diseases are spread – and how they can be controlled. An unhealthy majority, for example, seemed unaware that there is an important difference between an 'infectious' disease (spread through the environment – including by air) and a 'contagious' disease (spread by contact).

I quizzed a dozen doctors and nurses in a large NHS teaching hospital in Exeter, including several who had specific responsibilities for controlling the spread of infections such as MRSA and C.difficile and none of them seemed to me to understand the basic principles of disease spread.

Quite senior NHS personnel have tried to convince me that gastrointestinal infections are transmitted through the air and that this, not poor hygiene practises, explains why such bugs tend to sweep through hospital patients.

When I produced evidence showing that they were wrong (although it is possible for bugs to be transmitted via an aerosol route, the vast majority of infections are spread by poor hygiene) two members of NHS staff then tried to argue, apparently quite seriously, that bugs behaved differently in hospitals to the way they behaved elsewhere. One doctor insisted that bugs which are spread only by touch outside hospitals can be airborne inside hospitals. It is, perhaps, hardly surprising that staff don't bother to wash their hands and don't understand the importance of obeying the simplest rules about hygiene. And it is hardly surprising that the number of people dying from infections is rising dramatically. If you don't know how a disease is contracted you aren't likely to have much success in preventing its spread. Many doctors and nurses don't even seem to realise that common causes of vomiting, such as the norovirus, are spread largely through inadequate cleaning of contaminated wards.

I have, since the 1970s, been warning about the return of serious infections. The rise and rise of problems such as C.difficile and

MRSA was quite predictable. And other bugs will come back in a big way too. In my book *Paper Doctors* (1977) I pointed out that two things would result in a rise in infectious diseases: a lack of hygiene in hospitals and the abuse of antibiotics. I also predicted the rise in antibiotic-resistant infections.

In practice, avoiding infections such as MRSA and C.difficile is not difficult.

The best way to avoid them is to clean hospital wards and to persuade doctors, nurses and other members of staff to wash their hands in between seeing patients. But NHS hospitals are institutionally dirty. Public lavatories in France are cleaner than British hospitals. The area between beds is swept but the area under the beds is left dirty. Equipment is often filthy. Communal baths, showers and toilets are disgusting. Staff don't understand anything about hygiene. And no one cares.

Nothing is done about these problems because the complaints system is designed to protect the system rather than the patient. Hospitals are not interested in learning from their errors. They are only interested in denying the truth and avoiding responsibility. Medical records are kept not only to provide information but also with one eye on future litigation. One of the problems is that hospital staff (like other public service employees) are almost impossible to sack. When one former NHS chief executive was forced to resign her £150,000 a year job over Britain's deadliest superbug outbreak, she demanded a £150,000 pay off. The woman left her job after at least 90 patients died from C.difficile. And shortly after leaving her NHS job she set up a healthcare consultancy company (presumably, to tell the NHS how to improve hospitals). She set up the company with her partner who had quit a senior NHS job after the trust where he worked accumulated debts of £30 million. It seems that those who do leave the NHS are well compensated for their failure. And the concept of 'shame' seems as alien to the modern bureaucrat as the concept of 'duty' or 'responsibility'.

When the Healthcare Commission performed unannounced tests at 51 NHS Health Trusts, they found that nine out of ten of them had failed to meet hygiene standards put in place to reduce hospital infections. Two out of three hospitals did not complete a deep clean of their wards before a deadline set by the Government.

The result is that thousands of patients die every year in NHS hospitals because patients acquire lethal but avoidable infections. No one ever apologises. It is rare for anyone to be disciplined. Drivers go to prison if they are convicted of dangerous driving so why don't hospital staff go to prison for dangerous practices? If they did then I suspect that there would be far fewer unnecessary deaths in our hospitals. Twice as many Britons are killed by hospital infections as are killed on the roads. The total number of deaths from hospital superbugs such as MRSA and C.difficile is now well over 5,000 a year. The reason? Filthy wards, unhygienic practices, scandalously poor cleaning, grubby operating theatres and staff who never wash their hands. There are more such infections in British hospitals than anywhere else in the world. Why? British hospitals are dirtier than hospitals anywhere else in the world. Why? The staff in British hospitals are the most incompetent hospital staff in the world.

The rise in the incidence of superbugs is a phenomenon almost unknown outside the NHS and in my opinion it is a direct result of poor management and appallingly low standards of nursing. In the Middle Ages, patients used to keep out of hospitals whenever they could – knowing that a hospital stay could well prove fatal. Things aren't much different today. Most hospitals should have a Government health warning hanging over the front door. And the staff should have health warnings stamped on their foreheads. I wouldn't license most of them as abattoirs.

Since Ignaz Philipp Semmelweiss first demonstrated (in the mid-19th century) that deaths in the delivery room were caused by dirty hands, every child has been taught the importance of basic personal hygiene. Sadly, the message does not seem to have got through to the medical and nursing professions. Countless studies have shown that hospital staff just don't bother to wash their hands. A study of doctors' habits showed that two out of three anaesthetists failed to wash their hands before treating a new patient (even though anaesthetists frequently perform venepuncture surgery) while one in three surgeons did not wash their arms properly before an operation. At least one-third of all hospital infections are caused by dirty hands.

The cost of all this in simple financial terms is colossal.

Treating hospital contracted infections uses up around 15% of the hospital budget in the UK and adds around a week to each patient's hospital stay. The cost in human terms is incalculable: tens of thousands of patients die because of bugs they've caught from doctors, nurses, other staff or contaminated equipment. These aren't statistics: they are people. Real people. Every one of those unnecessary deaths is someone's wife, husband, mother, father, son, daughter, uncle, aunt, friend or neighbour. And remember, most of those patients die because doctors and nurses can't be bothered to wash their hands properly or because operating theatres aren't properly cleaned between operations.

The medical answer is – surprise, surprise – often to prescribe antibiotics, and a third of hospital patients end up taking them. It now takes 50 times as much penicillin to treat an infection as was required 30 years ago.

There is no doubt that antibiotic-resistant bacteria are now commoner in the UK because of the sloppiness in NHS hospitals as well as the bad prescribing habits of doctors.

It is hardly surprising that people who stay at home to be treated – or who go home quickly after day-case or short-stay surgery – usually get better much quicker than people who need long-stay treatment and who have to go into hospital.

It is because NHS hospitals are so filthy that there are more food related infections in the NHS than in the seediest, most disreputable restaurants. Hospitals which are home to rats and cockroaches (as many NHS hospitals are) are an excellent breeding ground for bugs of all sorts. Dirty hospitals are dirty because they are badly managed and because the staff are lazy or incompetent.

Attempts to deal with this embedded problem range between pathetic and laughable. An NHS hospital in Buckinghamshire was reported to have recorded a rap song to help staff learn how to wash their hands. The song apparently included the lyrics: 'Now clean between your fingers, just in case the bad bug lingers'. The hospital produced a video in which nurses wearing back to front baseball caps and bling jewellery stamped along to the beat. This was not a Christmas party joke and nor was it intended for children. This was a serious attempt to teach NHS staff how to wash their hands.

Nurses have even called for a vaccine to stop hospital infections spreading. It is, I suppose, easier to give a vaccine than to wash your hands.

The real problem is that hospital staff just don't seem to understand how infections spread.

For example, it is common to see nurses in shops still wearing their uniforms, complete with dubious looking stains. Nurses who wear their uniforms out of the hospital environment are showing just how ignorant they are. Bugs are transferred both ways. Nurses bring dangerous antibiotic-resistant bacteria out into the community and they take infections back into the hospital with them. Nursing staff should change their clothes whenever they leave the hospital where they work. And doctors working in hospital should always wear freshly laundered white coats.

There is now no doubt that infections are a major killer in our State hospitals. Watch the cleaners at work and you'll see them slide a mop down the centre of the ward. It's known in the mop wielding business as 'taking the mop for a walk'. They then wander off into their staff room for a tea break. And then serve patients their food. Staggeringly, the same people who clean the ward then serve patients their food. No one seems to see anything odd in this. The cleaners do not, of course, wash their hands between these two activities.

Cleaning staff (sorry, I think they now have to be called 'housekeepers') do not appear to have been told that they too must obey the basic rules of hygiene. The Government would save far more lives if it took down speed cameras and, instead, put up cameras in hospitals to check that nurses, cleaners and doctors wash their hands properly. Such a simple action would save billions of pounds and thousands of lives a year. Nurses who are spotted moving from patient to patient without washing their hands should be fired and banned from ever working in health care again.

The bad news is that things are going to get much, much worse I'm afraid. If Health and Safety operatives really want to save lives they should stop worrying about irrelevant 'health threats' and concentrate all their efforts on NHS hospitals.

In the future, two things are likely to happen.

First, the number of serious, deadly infections in our hospitals will rise. There will be periods when the infections will appear to be under control. But they will not be. Our hospital staff are institutionally lazy. Incompetence and ignorance are defended, protected and rewarded with promotion.

Second, the superbugs will escape from hospitals and start to kill people in their homes and places of work. It is already happening.

Medical officers in Holland have found that 50% of Dutch farmers are carrying a new strain of MRSA that is passed from hormone-fed pigs to humans. Already, a new, more virulent strain of MRSA has been found in the community. And the number of elderly people killed in care homes by the superbug C.difficile has officially tripled in the last two years. (Since killer bugs are often not mentioned on death certificates, the true figure is undoubtedly far higher than this.) This sad development is hardly surprising when one considers that nurses and local authority personnel who have responsibility for standards in care homes were trained in our hospitals.

A new mutant superbug, a new variety of E.coli resistant to antibiotics, has been found among cattle on a dairy farm in the north of England. It was the first time the particular strain of the bug had been found in Britain and it was only the third time the bug had ever been found anywhere in the world.

A Government spokeswoman said that 'no additional precautions are warranted'.

Says it all, doesn't it?


# IMMIGRATION

Most politicians are keen on immigration because they know that their home-grown population is ageing. Moreover, as the number of citizens of pensionable age is getting bigger so birth rates are falling. Politicians favour immigration as a way of lowering the average age and bringing in ready-made workers. They welcome the fact that immigrants tend to come with a high birth rate.

The resultant enforced and largely unwelcome mass immigration has altered societies throughout Europe; it has crushed cultures and great cities such as London and Paris have been destroyed by an unbearably and intolerably large influx of immigrations. There has inevitably, and predictably, been a rise in patriotism and nationalism.

All this immigration has been unnecessary because the aged need not be a burden. Many of those who have reached pensionable age want to keep working – and are perfectly capable of doing good and useful work. Most have extremely marketable skills. Most need to work. Most have been forced to give up work solely because of their age.

The solution is simple enough even for politicians to understand: allow all pensioners to work if they want to and punish anyone who forces an over 65-year-old into retirement against their wishes.

And lo and behold!

The need for immigrants (and the massive cultural disruption they bring) would immediately disappear.


# INFLATION

Inflation is terribly important to pensioners for the excellent reason that many who are retired will be living either on a fixed income or an income which rises according to its government's inflation figures.

Inflation is much loved by politicians because it helps get rid of government debt but it is a dangerous enemy for those whose income does not rise as rapidly as the real cost of living.

The problem is that people who have retired and who are living on a pension or on their savings are forced to live subject to the integrity of politicians.

Naturally, that is not terribly good news because governments everywhere lie about the inflation figures.

On the one hand, politicians want inflation to be high because when money is losing its value the Government's debts are gradually eradicated. (If the Government owes £5 and the value of money halves in a decade then, in ten years' time, the Government will still owe £5 but the £5 of debt will only cost £2.50 to repay.)

But politicians also need inflation to be low because pensions (both those which are statutory and those which are paid to former State employees such as civil servants, teachers, policemen and health care professionals) are usually inflation linked. The higher the inflation figures are, the more the Government has to pay out in pensions.

By and large, the need to pretend that inflation is low is greater than the need to make it higher.

And so governments fiddle the inflation figures to keep them low.

Fiddling the inflation figures, and keeping them artificially low, has a useful side effect. Because it deprives the elderly of money, it ensures that large numbers of them die of the cold. Please don't assume that this is a cynical or whimsical comment. Governments really do want to kill off old people. As far as politicians are concerned, the elderly are nothing more than an expensive nuisance.

As a general rule, the real rate of inflation is usually twice what your Government says it is. Sometimes it is three or four times as high as your Government tells you.

This means that people who are trying to live on a pension (even one which is nominally inflation proofed) will become poorer as the years go by.

It is important to be aware of this so that you can try to plan ahead. Someone who retires at 65 and whose income is only an inflation linked pension will find their buying power falling quite noticeably over the coming years.

It is very easy for government employed economists and statisticians to fiddle the official inflation figures. They calculate the official inflation figures by looking at the prices of the items in an imaginary 'basket' of commonly purchased things and services. And they fiddle the figure by picking the contents of that 'basket' very carefully.

So, for example, in the UK the Government has decided that most of us spend very little on housing costs, taxes (including local taxes), water, gas, electricity, petrol, bread, beer or insurance and so they think it is entirely reasonable to exclude all these expenses when the inflation figures are being prepared.

The Government claims that the inflation index is based on the rise in the cost of things which we buy regularly.

As I write, here are the items which the British Government has decided that the citizens of England, Scotland, Wales and Northern Ireland now regularly purchase and which must therefore be included in the official basket of commonly purchased items: canned apple cider, bottles of fruity cider, bicycle helmets, gin and almond milk

So, that's it.

I don't buy any of those things. And if you don't then someone, somewhere must be regularly buying a hell of a lot of canned cider, almond milk and bicycle helmets.

Fiddling the inflation figures is terribly easy.

One thing is clear: when planning ahead you must remember that your savings and your pension income will rarely, if ever, keep up with real inflation. Since you will be retired and will have no trade union to defend your financial interests, you will, therefore, have to dip into your savings in order to buy boring stuff like food and in order to heat your home.

The message here is a clear one: when you are planning your retirement you must try to organise things so that you can live on less than your pension income.

This will have two advantages. It will mean that as the years go by you will be able to spend a little more of your income. And it will mean that the savings you have made (albeit modest) can be put on one side to help pay for luxuries such as light bulbs and shoe repairs.


# INTELLIGENCE

Anyone who tells you that intelligence falters with age is a liar.

It may be true that old people don't do as well as children when taking intelligence tests but this is because intelligence tests are designed to measure the individual's ability to do well on intelligence tests.

Most intelligence tests are badly designed and equivocal and they most certainly do not test intelligence.

The fact is that older people may be slower to jump to conclusions than young people but they are just as bright as young people. In an experiment conducted in Australia, a class of 70-year-olds learned German at the same rate, and with the same level of success, as 15-year-olds.

In addition, older people are blessed with more knowledge and more experience.

It is, however, a sad fact of life that people who are told that they will become stupid when they get old tend to behave as they are instructed.

# J

## JARGON

Doctors often use a private code when writing medical notes about patients. They do it partly to save time and partly so that patients won't know what they have written. Just in case you get a chance to look at your medical records here are some of the abbreviations which are most commonly used these days. (Though do remember that not all these abbreviations are used in all hospitals).

NOD = Nice old duck
ACD = A complete dickhead
FAS = Fat and silly
NQOC = Not quite our class
RATTPO= Reassured and told to piss off
SITH = Soft in the head
BOAJ = Bit of a jerk
KSI = Knows someone important
PITB = Pain in the bum
SAD = Smelly and demented

If you find these abbreviations as offensive as I do, why not fight back? Here are two sets of abbreviations that you could try scribbling against your doctor's name in retaliation:
JUSLTIAWC = Jumped up spotty little twerp in a white coat
POFIAS = Pompous old fart in a suit
   I'm sure you'll be able to think of more.

# K

## KIDNEYS

Kidneys work best when supplied with fairly large quantities of fluid. Bottled spring water is better and safer than the stuff which comes out of your tap (which probably contains a potentially toxic collection of prescription drug residues).


## KNEES

Knee joints often become a little tricky when they are elderly and worn. You may be tempted to have surgery.

Unless my knees become unbearably painful, I will put up with the discomfort and use a walking stick for any extra support which is necessary. Knee operations seem to go wrong quite often.

# L

## LEARNING

Learning new stuff is as easy for 90-year-olds as it is for 20-year-olds. Both groups are slower than 10-year-olds. The more learning you do, the easier it gets.

## LEGACY

Politicians and people in public life are always worried about their 'legacy'. But what sort of legacy do most of them leave behind when they go to the great bragging shop in the sky? A war? A few bits of legislation which will be out of date and replaced within a year or two? A building which will be knocked down? A statue which will provide target practice for the pigeons?

Artists leave paintings but how many of those will still be hanging on walls in fifty years' time?

Writers leave books, but how many of those will last beyond a generation?

The best legacy is the respect and love of those whom you knew – those who knew you and who can rejoice in the memory of your life.

If you want to create a legacy then create one for the immediate, short-term future and build it out of love and kindness rather than bricks or paint.

## LEISURE

Most people demand and expect plenty of free time – away from work.

But many of them don't have the faintest what to do with their free time. They find it impossible to entertain themselves.

And so a huge leisure industry has developed – charging good money for often dull and pointless, time-consuming entertainments.


# LONGEVITY

It is myth that we are all living much longer. It is a thesis which is very convenient (doctors and drug companies take full advantage of it) but it is, nevertheless, a myth.

Of course, it is perfectly true that there are more old people around today than there were a century ago.

But this isn't because clever doctors and pill manufacturers have found ways to help us live longer.

There are two very simple reasons why we seem to be living longer.

First, the population is bigger.

When the population is greater, the chances are that there will be more old people. There are more old people living in London than there are old people living in Ross-on-Wye because there are more people living in London than there are people living in Ross-on-Wye.

Second, infant mortality is much lower today than it was a few decades ago. In England in 1900, one in four children didn't reach their 11th birthday. Many died as babies. Others died in childhood. Today less than one in 100 children fails to reach their 11th birthday. And, as a result, life expectation seems to have improved dramatically. This isn't difficult to explain. Imagine you have a family consisting of four people. One dies at the age of three. One dies at the age of 97. One dies at 30. And the fourth dies at 70. The four individuals have lived to 200 between them. Their average lifespan is 50 years. Now assume that the child who died at the age of three lives to 103. That will push up the average lifespan to 75 years.

A century or so ago, many newborn babies never saw their first birthday.

They were killed, largely, by infectious diseases.

Cholera, smallpox and typhoid killed millions.

The big change that has taken place has involved not doctors but better sewage facilities, cleaner water supplies, more spacious homes, more food and better built towns and cities.

All these things have helped slash infant mortality rates.

And so people *seem* to be living longer.

The drug industry and the medical profession are guilty of creating a new version of the post hoc ergo propter hoc fallacy. (Because B happened after A then B was caused by A.)

Doctors and drug company executives argue that adults live healthier lives (a lie) and live longer (another lie) because of developments made by the drug industry.

It would be just as reasonable if the shoe industry claimed that people live healthier lives, and live longer, because of developments made in the shoe industry.

Any improvements in health which have taken place in the last hundred years are a result of:

An increase in our understanding of, and ability to counteract, the way that infections such as cholera are spread (a 19th century development).

The provision of clean water supplies and better sewage facilities. (A 19th century development)

A reduction in infant mortality (a result of 19th century developments)

The introduction of antibiotics (an early 20th century development)

Safer surgery through antiseptics and anaesthesia (a 19th century development)

Today, however, longevity is falling, not because we have reached the limits of human life (we haven't) but because an increasing number of older citizens are being killed by doctors and nurses. Thousands more are dying of infections which are resistant to antibiotics.

Moreover, the incidence of disability among the elderly has been increasing steadily. Tomorrow's pensioners will be nowhere near as fit as their ancestors were.

Our fat and toxin rich diet has led to a steady increase in the incidence of cancer, obesity, heart disease, arthritis and many other causes of long-term disability.

Mental illness such as chronic anxiety and depression are now endemic.

And the powerful drugs which are prescribed by doctors with such careless enthusiasm have also produced a good deal of illness.

# M

## MEANS TESTING

Politicians are talking about taking the State pension away from people who have savings on which they can live.

State pensions are a not a luxury or a favour. They are an entitlement. They are paid for.

What is going to be next?

Are insurance companies going to refuse to pay out because they think you've got enough money? Are the slightly better off elderly going to be banned from using the roads or calling the fire brigade?

Means testing always stinks.

## MEMORIES

As we age so we tend to look backwards with fondness.

Sometimes this enthusiasm for the past is justified.

As we get older, we learn to worry more and our intrusive society, together with social media, has added a whole range of new threats and fears to our lives.

Escaping into the past can be relaxing and can help reduce stress.

But it is important to realise that sometimes we look back with rose coloured lenses in our retrospectoscope.

We naturally airbrush out the bad stuff so that that our younger days appear endlessly carefree.

## MENTAL ENERGY

Mental energy lasts well into old age, though physical energy may fall.

Old people who appear to have lost their get up and go are probably drugged.

## MIDDLE AGE

Middleagers sometimes panic as they see old age approaching and see how the elderly are ignored and mistreated.

## MINISTER

Britain has a minister to look after women's interests but there is no Minister for the Elderly, although the elderly are, without any doubt, the most oppressed minority group in the country.

In the absence of any other offers, I am appointing myself to the post.

And this book is my manifesto.

## MOTOR CARS

A driving licence, and a car, are essentials for those elderly individuals who live in rural areas.

Older drivers are much, much safer on the roads than young ones but doctors, police and the driving licencing authorities tend not to like older drivers being on the roads and will, often for no rational reason, leap at the chance to take away an older driver's licence.

Many older citizens who have clean driving licences are reluctant to have their eyes tested (or visit their doctor) lest an officious moron spot some minor abnormality and write to the authorities, who then take away their licence – forcing them to go through the humiliation and tiresome pain of taking another test or trying to survive without private transport in a world where public transport is patchy at best.

This is usually blatant prejudice.

Just imagine the fuss if the authorities decided to take driving licences away from blacks, women or gays simply because they were black, female or gay. Twats on social media would become hysterical.

The fact is that drivers over the age of 70 or so are much safer than younger drivers because the bad, bad drivers among them are dead, in prison or disqualified.

Insurance companies should, but rarely do, provide older drivers with cheaper premiums.

It is, in reality, the under 25-year-olds who are dangerous and should be taken off the roads en masse.

Losing their driving licence can be disastrous for many older people. If you live in a rural area you will need a car or the money to pay for taxis. Bus services in rural areas are at best appalling and at worst non-existent and are never likely to get any better.

# N

## NATIONAL HEALTH SERVICE

Britain's National Health Service died when matrons and almoners disappeared and were replaced by ranks of dull, greedy, self-serving bureaucrats with neither passion nor caring in their bones.

## NORMAL PRESSURE HYDROCEPHALUS

Many patients who are diagnosed as suffering from dementia, and who are stuffed into bed and left there to die, are actually suffering from a disorder known as normal pressure hydrocephalus which is quite curable.

The failure to diagnose normal pressure hydrocephalus is one of the biggest health scandals of the last 50 years.

Millions of patients have been wrongly diagnosed as suffering from Alzheimer's Disease, other forms of dementia or Parkinson's disease and, since there is no known cure for any of these disorders, they have been more or less abandoned by the medical profession and by society.

However, studies suggest that between five and ten per cent of all individuals diagnosed as suffering from Alzheimer's Disease or dementia are actually suffering from normal pressure hydrocephalus; a disorder which can produce similar symptoms – but which can be treated.

Around the world there are estimated to be nearly 50 million people suffering from dementia or Alzheimer's disease. One half of all the patients admitted to nursing homes are suffering from dementia of one sort or another. Millions of other patients who have been diagnosed with dementia of one kind or another are being looked after by their families. Many family members have had to abandon their jobs and their normal lives in order to find the necessary time. Millions more patients have been dumped in hospitals and nursing homes where they sit or lie, waiting to die. No one knows how many millions of undiagnosed individuals are struggling to cope with dementia, either alone or with the help of relatives, friends and neighbours.

Despite many promises, there is still no cure for dementia or Alzheimer's disease, nor is there any sign of one, but normal pressure hydrocephalus can be cured completely, quickly and with a simple, relatively cheap operation.

Normal pressure hydrocephalus is bizarrely under-researched, under-diagnosed and under-treated. There is almost certainly no disease affecting large numbers of people which is less understood.

Doctors certainly do not take the disorder as seriously as they should. Within the medical profession it is known (when it is known at all) as the 'wet, wacky and wobbly disease' – more a childhood term of abuse than a phrase redolent with respect. Many doctors have never even heard of it. Organisations which specialise in caring for the elderly are often appallingly ignorant about the disease, as are health websites.

On the internet, I asked the questions 'Why are old people unstable?' and 'Why do old people fall so often?' and none of the first several dozen responses mentioned 'normal pressure hydrocephalus'. In the UK, the NHS Choices website devotes less than 70 words to the disease and describes the condition as 'uncommon' which is manifest nonsense since it affects millions and is undoubtedly the commonest treatable cause of major disability and mental incapacity among the elderly.

Researchers are not interested in investigating the disease because a cure is already available and, since there is no need for a 'wonder drug' there are not going to be any big, fat grants from drug companies. And doctors are not interested in diagnosing or treating the disease because it invariably involves older patients, and doctors are encouraged by governments (and much of society) not to take much interest in elderly patients.

If you made a list of the 100 commonest, potentially fatal but most easily cured medical conditions which are most often mistakenly diagnosed as something else, then normal pressure hydrocephalus would be top of the list.

The only things we know for certain are that normal pressure hydrocephalus is terribly common, it produces devastating results, it is usually mistaken for something else and it is treatable. Patients who have been stuck in bed or in wheelchairs can, after treatment, get up and walk. They can resume their lives; talking and enjoying work and hobbies. Patients who have been abandoned have their lives back again.

A diagnosis of dementia (whether Alzheimer's or any other variety of dementia) can be devastating to a patient and to family and friends. But that diagnosis is often wrong. And if the correct diagnosis is normal pressure hydrocephalus then the true cause of the dementia is treatable.

The first sign that a patient may have normal pressure hydrocephalus is unsteadiness. Patients fall for no discernible reason. The second sign is developing dementia. The third sign is urinary incontinence.

It's important to catch the disease early. Any elderly patient who falls a good deal should be investigated for normal pressure hydrocephalus.

If a friend or relative is diagnosed with dementia then you should not accept the diagnosis until doctors have confirmed that the patient is not suffering from normal pressure hydrocephalus. If the treatment is started early then the outlook is good.


## NURSES

Many nurses are good, honest, hard-working and professional. But many are not. And it can be deadly to make the mistake of assuming that all nurses can be trusted.

An astonishing (and horrifying) survey conducted among readers of the journals *Nursing Standard* and *Nursing Older People* showed that five out of six nurses would, at least sometimes, fail to report abuse of the elderly people they were being paid to look after.

So, in my view, five out of six of nurses aren't fit to be nurses.

Would these same nurses ignore the abuse of children so easily? I suspect not.

This is utterly appalling and an indictment of the modern nursing profession.

The same survey showed that six out of ten nurses would say nothing if they knew that an elderly patient or care home resident was being beaten, bullied or robbed.

Why are nurses failing their patients?

One reason is cowardice.

Unbelievably, it seems that nurses are frightened to report abuse in case they themselves are abused by the person doing the abuse.

Oh, please.

Another reason is, apparently, 'fear of misinterpreting the situation'.

What sort of political correct garbage is that?

Hospital patients and nursing home residents now often suffer malnutrition and dehydration, abuse and rough treatment, lack of privacy, neglect, poor hygiene and bullying. Thousands and thousands of elderly people are left for hours in soiled clothes.

How can anyone 'misinterpret' any of that?

And *why?*

I'll tell you why.

It is because too many modern nurses are lazy, stupid and incompetent. Too many are far too self-important to do anything other than stare at a computer screen all day long.

In my view, nurses who say nothing when they see abuse are as guilty as the abusers. A once great profession is, today, in a worse state than it was in the days of Dickens.

Is it so very old-fashioned of me to believe that every nurse should always report every incident of abuse?

Always. Without exception.

# O

## OFFICIALS

Officials are paid by us to work for us but many consider it their job to make life difficult, to delay normal processes and to waste our time.

If you find yourself obstructed, frustrated or annoyed by any official, do not hesitate to make a formal complaint. These days there is always a complaints system and the chances are that if you make a formal complaint there will be a lengthy investigation which will not do the official's career any good at all.


## OLD FOLKS' HOMES (see also CARE HOMES, NURSING HOMES, RESIDENTIAL HOMES, PRISONS, ZOOS and MIGHT AS WELL BE LOCKED IN A CUPBOARD UNDER THE STAIRS)

Survey after survey has shown that the elderly in care homes and hospitals are ignored and treated worse than animals on a factory farm. Many residents are drugged and kept in bed so that they are less trouble. Compliant local doctors provide the drugs. Willing nursing auxiliaries or completely unqualified members of staff serve up the tablets as prescribed. It is rare to find anyone working in one of these homes who speaks good English. For this the fee is usually a minimum of between £30,000 and £50,000 a year. If you want to rent a bed in a good home where people are likely to show a little caring you can expect to pay considerably more.

Most of these homes are appalling but thankfully, 95% of old people live at home and pretty well look after themselves.

Most people in retirement or old folks' homes could live at home too. Many are pushed into residential care by well-meaning relatives who worry too much about their welfare.

The fact is that if you want to have your meals and laundry done for you, go and live in a hotel. It will be cheaper, the food will be better and the staff will be nicer to you. Go somewhere nice, maybe by the seaside, and you will be far better off than in a smelly old folks' home. If you want sunshine, move to a hotel in Spain. There you will probably find that everyone speaks English. There will be fewer absurd rules too.

And do not assume that the care will be better in an old folks' home than in a hotel.

One of the major problems with many private nursing homes is the shortage of suitable staff. Like most doctors, I know of patients who needed only simple nursing care who have died in nursing homes, simply because there were not enough nurses around to ensure that wounds were attended to, that pressure sores were looked after or that pills were given. If you have 30 patients in a home and each patient takes 20 tablets a day (by no means unusual) that means that 600 tablets must be given out to the right patients at the right time every day of the week. Without enough nurses that alone can be a daunting task. Patients may be given their sleeping tablets early in the evening so that the staff can get off home. The elderly man or woman who is restless at night may be put into a cot bed and then left there all night. If the patient concerned needs to pass water during the night, as so many old people do, he or she will be unable to get up to do so. The nurses will come to the conclusion that the patient is incontinent and the downhill slide will have begun.

When there are not enough nurses in a home, things can deteriorate quickly. The staff can quickly get depressed and short-tempered and the residents will suffer.

If you must go into a care home or a nursing home of some kind, there are some fairly simple ways in which you can assess the suitability of a nursing home.

You will want to choose a home which is in a suitable area – ideally close enough for friends and relatives to visit easily and close enough to a town for fit individuals to get out and about.

If possible, you should choose a home which allows residents to take with them a reasonable selection of their own belongings, including furniture. Many old people settle into a new home much more quickly when they are allowed to take with them familiar furniture and souvenirs. The bedrooms in some nursing homes are packed with old photographs, curios and nicknacks. I am sure that it is no coincidence that in these homes, where each room has a personality of its own, the residents always seem far more cheerful than in those homes which are spick and span and characterless.

Some homes allow old people to take pets with them, and this may be an important consideration. I once visited a nursing home where there were more cats than people, and though the whole house reeked of cats, the residents seemed to be as happy as if they were in heaven.

Be suspicious of places which have prefabricated buildings in the garden. This always suggests that the owners are trying to get as many guests as they can into the house. There will probably be a shortage of loos, bathrooms and dining accommodation.

Here then are some final things to check when looking for a nursing home:

1) Check that the home is properly registered.

2) Ask for details of the total weekly rates, including any extras.

3) Ask about the availability of doctors. Patients may only be accepted in some homes if they are on a local doctor's list. Make sure that there is a system for calling a doctor in an emergency.

4) Make sure that there is a call system in all bedrooms and that there are enough telephones.

5) Check that there is a qualified nurse on duty 24 hours a day, 365 days a year. You should ask about the number of nurses employed. If there isn't a nurse permanently available then it may be cheaper to find a hotel.

6) Ensure that the home provides the sort of total care needed. The atmosphere is important. The home does not need to have expensive paintings hanging on the walls, but it should be clean and bright and smell good. Visitors should be allowed into the home fairly freely. Some homes even have spare rooms available for the use of visiting relatives who have travelled a long way to see someone.

7) Check that the building is safe and that there is an adequate fire escape.

8) Ask whether a chiropodist calls and whether a physiotherapist is available when needed.

It is probably a good idea to visit a potential nursing home at a meal-time. You can not only see what sort of food is served but also learn a lot from how it is served. Is there anyone to help those residents who cannot cut their own food easily? Or are meal-times hectic?

If the staff cannot cope with your visit, how could they cope with a real emergency?

If the person showing you round objects when you ask questions, then ask more questions. If he or she explodes with anger, you can be sure that he/she does not have the patience to deal with old people who may be confused and difficult.

Remember that anyone who runs a private nursing home is trying to make money. There is absolutely nothing wrong with that. But how much money are they trying to make and how quickly and honourably and honestly are they trying to make it?

As an alternative to nursing homes and hospitals, there are many flats and houses available which were built especially for the elderly and which are equipped with many specially designed labour-saving gadgets. It is usual for these flats to have a warden on the site who can keep an eye on the infirm and help with some chores occasionally. The availability of such flats varies from area to area and it is important to choose a flat carefully. The flat should, preferably, be specifically designed for use by an elderly person, with smooth floor surfaces and an easy-to-run kitchen. If the flat is a tower block, then the tower should have a lift. The flat should be not too far from the shops or the bus service, but preferably not too close to a busy road or school.

In addition to flats there are, in many areas, alms-houses which are let out to elderly people at low rents. Often these alms-houses are run by private organisations, sometimes organisations with religious affiliations. Sadly, however, the demand for these always seems greater than the supply.

# P

## PARANOIA

Paranoia is entirely justifiable among those over 65 – even 60. The truth is that 'they' do want you dead. All politicians and bureaucrats are your enemy. They want you out of the way because in their terms you are an unproductive liability.

And I'm afraid that most health care workers are your enemy too. Any profession which can dismiss the frail elderly as 'bed blockers' is the enemy.

## PATRONISING

I have 17,564 pet hates.

Here is one.

I'm on the telephone talking to some kid and he insists that before we go any further he must know my birth date. This is a modest nod in the direction of security. I tell him my birth date. 'That's brilliant', says the patronising kid when I get my date of birth right. He then asks me my postcode. That's part two of the security process though since it is one of the most public pieces of knowledge on the planet one has to wonder at its value. 'Wonderful! Marvellous!' he says when I get my postcode right. Patronising little bastard.

There's plenty of other stuff too.

Advertisers take the piss out of the elderly without a second thought.

If advertisers want to poke fun at someone then the first choice will be an elderly, white man. The second choice will be an elderly white woman.

No advertiser would ever dare take the mickey out of a Muslim, a Scot or a man of any age wearing a Jewish skullcap.

And then there's the stuff in between the adverts on television.

On chat and game shows, hosts and interviewers always lower their voices when they talk to anyone with one or two grey hairs.

'And how old are you?' they ask, in the sort of tone they also favour when talking to backward children, and the very careful enunciation they favour when talking to the deaf, the blind, the backward and the foreign.

The reply, assuming that the guest turns out to be over 60, will be greeted with gasps of delight and awe and the host will lead the live audience in a round of applause.

It's all so excruciatingly patronising.

Can you imagine television hosts asking a guest what religion they are?

'I'm a Methodist, Amanda.'

'Oh how wonderful. Marvellous. Congratulations.'

Big condescending smile and much applause.

If you are ever asked your age by a television host then reply: 'You tell me how old you are, Simon, and I'll tell you how old I am.'

I also get pissed off by colleges which run courses for the elderly (designed to help 'older citizens' understand computers or learn to paint).

Can you imagine the outcry if special courses were organised for Jews or homosexuals or black people?

'Special course in using Windows 91 for black people.'

'Enrol now in our art classes for people of the Jewish persuasion.'

They'd never dare, would they?

So, what gives the miserable bastards the feeling that they can patronise older folk?

And finally, it is has now become popular to put pre-school children into retirement homes so that the decrepit old folk therein will benefit from the association. The idea is that the oldsters play games with the children and thereby regain their youthful attitudes. This, surely, is the most utterly patronising idea of all time. The residents of retirement homes need to be treated with respect not humiliated in this grotesque way. The woeful morons who thought this one up should be executed for initiating a crime against humanity.

# PEAK PENSIONER

Depending on where you live, between a fifth and a quarter of the population is now over the age of 65. And since birth rates are falling, the percentage of older folk in most communities is rising rather rapidly.

And we haven't yet reached what I have decided to call 'Peak Pensioner', though this phenomenon is one much feared by politicians, who are always eager to share their fear about the rising number of older folk in our society and to use the increase in the number of over 65s as an excuse for encouraging unfettered immigration.

The good thing is that the more of us there are, the more clout we have.

If we stick together we could control the country.

Here is to Pensioner Power!


# PENSIONS

There comes a time in everyone's life when they realise they are getting older. They find they need reading spectacles when faced with small print. Their hair gets thinner and doesn't need cutting quite as often. Hills suddenly become steeper. Stairs go on for longer.

At the age of about 50, pensions, which always used to be as dull as plumbing and emergency drains cover, suddenly seem enormously practical, very relevant and painfully important.

And as the official retirement age looms, so folk begin to worry about becoming redundant – in every sense of the word.

And then there's the money.

Or the shortage of money.

When reality hits, it often seems clear that retirement isn't going to be endless games of golf, sailing into the sunshine and taking expensive trips around the world on luxury cruise ships.

Instead the size of a pension becomes something to worry about.

Will it be eaten up by inflation? Will there be enough to pay for keeping warm and buying a little food occasionally?

We all know that basic, background costs (council rates, utility bills, insurance, heating) have all soared and that such fripperies aren't included in the official inflation figures.

Before you reach retirement age try living for a week on your pension.

Will you cope? Or do you need to delay your retirement or find another job?

## PERKS OF AGE

There are some perks in being old.

Cancer tends to grow more slowly than it does in younger people, so that's a good thing, and something definitely worth looking forward to.

The big, nasty utility companies aren't supposed to cut you off without a therm (especially if the weather is bad). They are supposed to give you a week or two's notice at the very least.

And if you do get sent to prison, you're far less likely to be gang raped or beaten up. No 70-year-old is going to be someone's bitch. Beating up a 70-year-old isn't going to enhance the reputation of the prison hard man is it?

## PILLS

When I was working as a doctor, I often saw patients who were struggling to take 60 or 70 pills a day. On occasion, I saw patients who were taking over 100 tablets and capsules every single day.

These patients had to take some pills in the morning, some in the evening, some four times a day, some three times a day, some six times a day, some when they needed them and doubtless some every now and then when the moon was in the right position.

The doctors who had prescribed such confusions of pills apparently did not realise that drugs often interact with one another – producing serious side effects.

Nor did they stop to think of the side effects all these drugs were likely to produce.

Indeed, many of the drugs were prescribed simply to counteract the side effects produced by other drugs.

And nor, apparently, did it occur to these idiot doctors that when you're given pills to take three times a day, four times a day and five times a day then you are bound to become slightly confused about which drug you've taken and which one is due to be taken next.

The diuretic, which needs to be taken first thing in the morning, gets swallowed at night, causing incontinence, and the sleeping tablet, which should be taken at night, is taken in the morning, producing day-long drowsiness and confusion.

When their unfortunate patient collapses in confusion, the idiot doctors diagnose dementia and prescribe another armful of pills.

If you are taking more than a dozen pills a day then you should ask your doctor to rationalise your drug taking regime.

You almost certainly don't need as many pills as you are taking. Ask your doctor to organise things so that you take pills three times a day or four times a day – and not both. If your doctor doesn't have the time or the inclination to help you then I suggest you dump him.

Make sure you know what each pill is for. The names of the pills will be on the bottles or packets so you can look them up on the internet. If you don't have access to the internet I don't blame you a bit – just find a kid over the age of three and ask them to do it for you.

Finally, I have to warn you not to stop taking pills which have been prescribed for you.

Some pills produce serious problems if they are stopped suddenly. And, who knows, there is always a chance that some of the drugs you have been prescribed may well be essential. Always talk to a doctor before stopping pills which have been prescribed for you.

# PRESCRIBING ERRORS

Prescription drugs can, and do, save many lives. But prescription drugs are one of the major killers in our modern world.

If drugs were only ever prescribed sensibly, and when they were likely to interfere with a potentially life-threatening disease, then the risks associated with their use would be acceptable.

But all the evidence shows that doctors do not understand the hazards associated with the drugs they use and frequently prescribe inappropriately and excessively. Many of the deaths associated with prescription drug use are caused by drugs which should not have been prescribed or which did not need to be taken. Patients are given the wrong drug. Or they are given the wrong dose of the right drug. Or they are given the right drug by the wrong route (for example, a drug that should be injected into a muscle may be injected directly into the bloodstream).

Experts believe that there is an error, roughly one in every eight times when a hospital patient is given a drug.

Since an ordinary hospital patient may receive a dozen different drugs – at different times of the day – the opportunities for error are colossal.

In a 300 bed hospital, there may be between 300 and 400 medication errors every day! Some of those errors will result in mild discomfort. Some will result in death.

So, before you take a prescription drug make sure you should be taking it. And make sure you know what it is for.

And if you are in hospital, then make sure that whoever is giving you a drug is certain that you are being given the right dose of the right drug at the right time.


# PROSTATE

The prostate gland always contains lumps of cells which look as if they may be cancerous but which probably don't need treating since the owner of the prostate will probably die of something else long before the funny looking cells in his prostate gland cause any serious problems.

You should be aware that prostate cancer awareness week campaigns are often promoted by companies making screening tests.

These tests are expensive.

And they produce a mass of false positives and false negatives.

The men with false positives think they have prostate cancer when they haven't. They will inevitably worry a great deal. Worse still, they may be treated unnecessarily by doctors and surgeons. The consequences can be catastrophic.

The men with false negatives walk away thinking, quite wrongly, that they are perfectly healthy and can happily ignore any physical signs which they might develop.

The bottom line is that the much promoted prostate cancer screening test has now been proven beyond doubt to be a dangerous waste of time and money which does far more harm than good.

If your doctor suggests that you have such a test, change your doctor because he is out of date and useless.

# Q

## QUACKS

Quacks, which is to say unqualified persons flogging medicaments which are of no value but around which a viable story can be spun, usually target the elderly.

They do this because older citizens, as a whole, tend to be more trusting, less wary and easier to part from their money than younger folk who are likely to be cynical and more difficult to cheat.

It's nice to know that the world is awash with confidence tricksters who delight in getting rich by tricking money out of the vulnerable, the susceptible and the lonely.

I wouldn't put these tricksters in prison. That costs us all money. I'd tie them to stakes in a snake pit and then fill the pit with the most venomous snakes I could find.

# R

## RACISM

They (media, celebs, politicians and advertisers) all take the piss out of white, elderly Englishmen in a way which they wouldn't dare ever do when talking about any other ethnic group.

Have you ever wondered why nearly all homeless tramps (apart from the imported ones) are single, white, ageing males?

It's because single, white, ageing males are bottom of all council housing lists.

## RECUPERATION

Recuperative powers weaken with age. This means that if you run a marathon at the age of 80, you will probably take longer to recover than you would have taken when you were 40.

## REFORMERS

Reformers want to alter the framework of society and the attitudes of people.

Today's pseudo-rebels (who are militant about their reforming) want society to change so that they get everything they want (and they want it now). They care nothing about the elderly who have become an under-privileged minority. Their motives are entirely selfish.

Many of the pseudo-rebels are students or unemployed and have not yet enjoyed or endured life as taxpayers. They know very little about the world and they want a more statist society. They want a world in which everything is paid for by someone else.

Their inexperience and ignorance, allied to a level of arrogance which means they do not consider it necessary for them ever to consult their elders (who they certainly do not regard as their betters), means that they are intent on creating a future which will ensure disaster for them, their children and their children's children.

So if we want to preserve the world we know, we oldies have to push back. We need to organise and become militant to defend

## REPEAT PRESCRIPTIONS

Repeat prescribing (allowing patients to collect prescriptions for their medication without seeing the doctor) was a good idea when it started.

The idea was that patients who needed long-term medication but who didn't need to see the doctor as often as they needed more pills, could simply collect their prescriptions in between consultations.

So, for example, patients with diabetes or epilepsy or high blood pressure or arthritis could see the doctor once every three or six months and pick up their prescriptions in between their visits. It was a good idea because it saved everyone time. And patients were told that they should only ask for, and collect, repeat prescriptions if they were happy that their symptoms were well controlled.

Today, the basic principles upon which repeat prescribing were founded have been forgotten. Patients ask for, and are given, repeat prescriptions for a whole range of disorders and some go for years without ever seeing a doctor.

Well over half of all the prescriptions doctors write are for patients they don't see. Every single day of the working week in the UK the best part of a million repeat prescriptions are collected from GP's surgeries – frequently by patients who never needed to be on drugs in the first place.

Back in the mid-1980s, I pointed out that Britain's huge tranquilliser and sleeping pill addiction problem had been caused largely by the growth in 'repeat prescribing'. Since then the only thing that has changed has been that the problem has got worse.

Patients and doctors both abuse a system that was originally a good idea but which is now a dangerous practice.

Not long ago, a GP was fined for continuing to issue repeat prescriptions for a patient who had died.

If you collect prescriptions without seeing your doctor, make sure that you visit the surgery at least once every three months to check that you still need to take the medication – and that it is still appropriate for your needs.

# RESPECT

Respect used to be a right. In what are considered to be the 'bad old days' it was generally agreed that we were all entitled to respect from everyone in our lives; whether they were permanent residents or just wandering through.

The elderly, in particular, were regarded as deserving of respect since they were the people in society who had survived the longest and experienced the most and whose wisdom was, therefore, the greatest.

Younger folk consulted older folk when things went wrong because they suspected (quite rightly) that whatever had gone wrong had probably gone wrong before.

Sadly, that attitude is now passé.

Today, the young are filled with more prejudices than ever, and most 20-year-olds assume (or in many cases 'know') that anyone over 70, 60 or even 50 must, by definition, be senile, sexless and stupid.

There is a widespread assumption that anyone over 50 is not entitled to any dignity or respect because their age means that they are inevitably and inescapably stupid, inept and dependent.

The millennials have spread the word: give no respect to anyone; no one gets respect automatically.

Moreover, in this new, modern world it is impossible to earn respect.

The only way to get it is to demand it.

# RESUSCITATION

At what age are patients simply allowed to die?

How old is too old for a patient to be resuscitated?

At what point does society have the right to say 'You've lived long enough, now you must die and make way for someone else'?

And why should resuscitation be decided by age? It is possible to argue that it would make as much sense to decide according to wealth or beauty.

But ageism is now officially accepted. Anyone over 60 is now officially old, though in a growing number of hospitals, the cut off age for resuscitation is 55.

It is wise to keep out of hospitals and away from doctors as much as possible.


# RETIREMENT

When retirement is a long way off, we tend to look on the idea rather fondly. It will be good to have time to spend on the things we really want to do. We can play golf every day and spend as long as we like in the bar afterwards. We can take up wood carving, painting or fell walking. We can learn to paint or we can study Russian.

In the event, of course, things don't often work out quite as expected.

Many retired folk become bored, dissatisfied, frustrated, restless and lonely.

And they are too short of money to be able to do all the things they dreamt of doing.

So why retire?

Most of those who have retired realise, within a few weeks, that they would have been happier if they had carried on working – even if they had worked shorter hours.

The days of forced retirement may have ended (officially) but many employers still make it clear that they expect employees to retire at 65. The ones who don't take the hint will often find themselves suddenly made redundant.

Oddly enough, senior judges and MPs (the ones who make the rules) never seem to retire.

If someone said 'You can't do your job because you are black, Christian, Muslim, Jewish, female, homosexual, transsexual or disabled, there would be outrage.

Politicians would be clubbing each other to death for a chance to denounce the someone who said it.

But it is apparently perfectly legal, proper and acceptable to say that someone can't do their job because they've had too many birthdays.

In truth, they may be just as capable as ever but they will be considered incapable not because of biology, not because of their age, but because of the role they are forced to play in our society: helpless and dependent.

(In our society, everyone seems to play the part they are expected to play. So doctors behave like doctors, policemen behave like policemen and professional footballers behave like professional footballers. There is a real danger that elderly people will behave like elderly people are expected to behave. )

The result of all this is that many oldsters believe that they are irrelevant, useless, superfluous and a nuisance – and not entitled to be treated like people.

They have been brainwashed in the way that blacks and women used to be brainwashed.

The bottom line is that most old folk like being retired and thrown out of useful employment in the same way that kids enjoyed being sent up chimneys and black slaves got a real kick out of picking cotton all damned day long, doo dah day.

If you don't want to retire you don't have to.

If they make you retire before you are ready then there's a good chance that you can force them to pay you compensation.


# RETIREMENT AGE

In the 1880s, Germany's Chancellor, Otto von Bismarck decided to prick the balloon of developing demands for a more socialist approach to politics, by introducing a State pension programme for older Germans who had stopped working.

Bismarck and the German Emperor William the 1st, argued before the Reichstag that people who had reached the age of 70 should receive a State pension. This was later reduced to 65 since 65 was, at the time, the average German life expectancy.

In Britain, the Old-Age Pensions Act of 1908 proposed a weekly pension of 5 shillings a week to the half a million citizens who were over the age of 70. Married couples received 7 shillings and 6 pence a week. The pension age was later lowered to the age of 65.

(The large number of individuals eligible for a pension will probably startle those who wrongly believe that until 2016, average life expectation was no more than 30 or so and that anyone surviving into their 50s was a freak worthy of a starring role in a fair, billed alongside the bearded lady and an obligatory dwarf.)

In 1935, Germany's proposed retirement age of 65 was selected for a retirement age in the US when President Franklin Roosevelt introduced the idea of State pensions into the US.

And the same age has, for years, been the generally accepted age at which workers could expect to retire and receive a pension.

It seems entirely reasonable that older people should be entitled to retire at some pre-determined age, should they wish to do so.

But although it seems equally unreasonable that many older people are forced to retire little or nothing is done to stop it happening. It is against the law in most civilised countries to force individuals to retire at a certain age. But that doesn't stop it happening.

# RIGHTS

Never forget that it's your body and your mind and, unless the professionals can prove that you are stark raving bonkers, it is up to you to decide what treatment to accept and what to refuse.

The medical establishment recently decreed that in future, patients should take the big decisions about their own treatment programmes.

I am delighted since this is something I have been advocating since the Hundred Years War.

Sadly, the medical establishment has not made this move because of my campaigns or because it thinks it is the right thing to do but because they believe that if patients make their own strategic decisions the number of lawsuits will fall because if or when things go wrong. They believe that doctors will be able to disclaim all responsibility and point the stodgy finger of blame at the patient.

Still, the means may be a bit dodgy but the end is definitely acceptable.


## ROLE PLAYING

Luck, money and genes affect how we age.

But we are also encouraged to play the part other people expect us to play.

We have a role imposed on us as we age.

We are expected to be, useless, unemployable, impoverished and grateful for any scraps of respect or dignity we are offered.

Bugger that.

I'll be satisfied with the respect and dignity the 25-year-old expects.

Nothing less.


## RUBBISH COLLECTING

Thanks to daft laws from the European Union, all householders in the UK are now forced to sort their rubbish and put it into lots of separate boxes and bags. There are rules about which stuff goes into which box and there are rules about when the boxes can be put out for collection.

All this is nonsense, of course.

Most of the stuff which has been sorted for recycling is sent to China or mainland Europe to be burnt or buried.

And putting waste food into little plastic boxes attracts rats and will eventually result in a recurrence of the plague and the Black Death.

If you find it difficult to manage the rubbish rules and to handle the heavy bins with which you have been provided, contact your local council and insist that you need help. Councils have a duty to provide whatever help you need in this regard.

# S

## SCIENCE

Don't believe anyone who tries to convince you that modern medicine is a science. It isn't. Despite all the money spent on medical research, doctors still don't know how long they should give antibiotics for (or what dose they should use). They guess.

And doctors invariably give the same dose of a drug to people of different ages and sizes. No one ever bothers to do clinical trials to find out whether drug dosages should be varied according to age and size. The result is that a 20-year-old woman weighing seven stone will be given the same dose of a drug as a 45-year-old man weighing 20 stone. And a 75-year-old woman will be given the same dose of a drug as an 18-year-old youth.

It's hardly science, is it?

## SCREENING

As you get older you will find yourself frequently invited to your doctor's surgery for a screening test or a health check. Don't make the mistake of thinking that your doctor suddenly cares for you. In Britain, family doctors are paid huge bonuses if they perform routine health checks on their elderly patients.

The principle of screening is a simple one: the patient trots along to the doctor and the doctor (for a chunky, great fee, of course) does tests which are designed to spot early signs of disease. The tests which are offered are done because the medical establishment has managed to convince NHS bureaucrats that screening is worth paying for.

Doctors are enthusiastic about screening because it's enormously profitable. And they're very lukewarm about encouraging their patients to follow healthier lifestyles because there is no money in it.

For decades now, just about every attempt to show that medical screening programmes save lives has proved that they are a waste of time, energy and money. Indeed, surveys have proved that, because of the risk of false positives, medical screening programmes do far more harm than good.

Medical screening programmes go back a long way.

The first recorded screening took place at a public brothel in Avignon in 1347 when a local Abbess and a surgeon examined all the working women every Saturday to see whether or not they were fit to carry on serving the local population.

Then, in 1917 large corporations in the U.S. thought it might be a good idea to have their employees examined regularly. When half of four million American men called up for military service during the First World War proved to be unfit for military service, insurance companies started screening the general population.

Since then, the medical screening business has grown virtually unchecked and those promoting screening (or health checks) merrily ignore the inconvenient fact that since the 1970s there has been ample evidence to show that medical screening programmes are not just a waste of time and money but can also be a serious health hazard.

Back in 1979, the World Health Organisation published a report which showed that people who were subjected to regular medical screenings needed to go to hospital more often but were not as healthy as people who did not undergo regular medical screenings. The conclusion was that health screening is expensive and ineffective.

In the same year, the results of a Canadian Task Force report on Periodic Health Examination came to the conclusion that annual medical check-ups should be abandoned since they were both inefficient and potentially harmful.

Health checks are harmful for many reasons.

First, when people are taught to put their faith in medical check-ups they tend to abandon responsibility for their own health and enjoy a false sense of security. Patients forget that a medical check-up is no more a sign of long-term health than an encouraging bank statement is a sign of permanent financial security. A patient who is given a clean bill of health is likely to ignore strange symptoms which develop a week or two later. And there is a danger that he (or she) may feel that it is unnecessary to eat wisely or to take regular exercise.

Second, screening examinations may frighten people. They can result in cancer phobias, neuroses and depression. And they can result in so much stress that the immune system is damaged – leading to a greater susceptibility to disease.

Third, the procedures involved in screening programmes may do physical harm. There are, for example, some doctors who perform coronary angiographs as part of their check-up procedures. As many as two patients per 100 may die during this procedure.

Fourth, when a screening examination results in a false positive the patient may be given a treatment which may damage his or health. A major Swedish report on breast screening (a type of screening which has been shown to be particularly useless and dangerous but enormously profitable) showed that out of 600,000 women screened, there had been 100,000 false positives. This means that 100,000 healthy women were told that they had breast cancer when they didn't have anything wrong with them. They were terrified and treated unnecessarily.

Fifth, screening is expensive. GPs are paid a fortune for conducting simple health checks (Actually, to be accurate, they are usually paid for telling their practice nurses, whose salaries are largely paid by taxpayers, to do the tests.)

Sixth it is a proven fact that screening doesn't work. It is dangerous and does far more harm than good.

Every independent survey I have found has concluded that screening (whether general or specific) is costly and useless. The reality is that the only people who benefit from screening programmes are doctors – and other parts of the health industry. Screening programmes are extremely profitable.

The problems, and hazards, with screening programmes seem boundless. For example, you have a one in three chance of a false positive result if you have a full body CT scan. There is also a one in 20 chance that the scan will miss signs of disease – and give you a false sense of complacency and encourage you to ignore important physical signs.

I've been screaming about the dangers of screening programmes for 30 years or more and was delighted when, in November 2009, the American Cancer Society finally accepted that screening for breast and prostate cancer is inefficient, inaccurate and alarmist and can do damage by detecting cancers that either don't exist or wouldn't kill if they did.

Naturally, however, such programmes are still promoted within the NHS where staff favour screening programmes because it is easy to measure the results. They can say: 'We screened 10,000 people and found 10 people with possible cancer. We, have, therefore, saved 10 lives.' In medical and statistical terms, such claims are nonsensical. But in political terms they are invaluable.

Offering sensible advice is much cheaper and safer but the results cannot be measured and it is difficult for the NHS to claim the credit for saving lives.


## SECRETS

I believe that medical confidentiality is vital. I also believe that you can't be a little bit confidential, any more than a woman can be a little bit pregnant.

Over a third of a century ago, I resigned as a GP when NHS bureaucrats tried to force me to write confidential information about my patients on sick notes.

I refused and was fined heavily for doing so. It seemed to me that this was a vital matter of principle.

Patients are entitled to believe that what they tell their doctors in confidence will remain confidential.

I felt that by putting diagnoses on sick notes (likely to be read by heaven knows how many people) I would be betraying that confidence.

And so I resigned from the NHS and became a full-time writer.

When I was a GP, I found that I was constantly having to find ways to defend my patients from the bureaucrats.

Once, for example, a State bureaucrat arrived and announced that he was going to take away all the medical records I held for my 2,500 patients. He had a van parked outside my surgery, ready to take the records away with him. I pointed out that this would be a breach of confidentiality and would endanger the lives of my patients. The bureaucrat wouldn't budge. He had a form giving him the right to remove the records for routine checking. He asked me to take a medical record file from its drawer and to read what was written in red on the bottom of the file. I did so. It said: 'The property of the Minister of Health'. Suddenly I remembered Shylock and the *Merchant of Venice*. 'You can take the records,' I told him. 'But you can't take the ink.' He stared at me, uncomprehendingly. 'The paper belongs to the Minister of Health,' I conceded. 'But the ink on the paper belongs to me. So you can take the records but you must leave the ink behind.'

He left.

Things today are rather different; they are worse, much worse

Today, patients can't trust their doctors to keep their secrets.

The General Medical Council has told doctors that they must 'share' their patients' secrets with just about anyone who asks for it. Naturally, there is no promise that the person to whom the information is given will not pass it on to their friends and neighbours.

So, the bottom line is that you can't trust a doctor to keep your secrets. Don't tell her or him anything you wouldn't be happy to see on her or his Facebook page.

# SENILITY

The word senile isn't a diagnosis – it is merely a term of abuse applied to people over 60 who dare to make a fuss. Modern folklore is that the old are inevitably stupid and incompetent and that if they must be tolerated then they must be kept in conditions which would not be tolerated for farm animals or prisoners, and they must be treated with plenty of contempt and absolutely no respect.

# SEX

There is a widespread feeling among younger folk that people over the age of 50 should not think of sex – let alone contemplate any practical activity.

Staff in residential homes and long-stay hospitals often seem to be deeply disturbed by any hint that a pair of their residents might want to develop a relationship, hold hands, go to bed together or get married. The two sexes are kept apart as carefully as school-children on a field trip.

This is patronising and ageist and it is, to put it politely, total bollocks.

# SHINGLES

I received an unsigned letter from our GP inviting me to make an appointment to have a shingles vaccination.

The vaccine was apparently being offered to selected groups of individuals over the age of 70 and is, no doubt, a result of determined efforts by the drug industry to find ways to make more money out of old people (an expanding market) as well as children (a market which is definitely not expanding quite so rapidly).

The letter from my GP contains no reference to side effects but told me that if I want more information I should consult the website www.shinglesaware.co.uk

What the GPs failed to point out is that www.shinglesaware.co.uk was set up by Sanofi Pasteur MSD which is (golly I can hardly believe this) a manufacturer of vaccines. Actually, to be more specific, it is the manufacturer of this very vaccine. So my GPs are using a vaccine manufacturer's website as the source of information about a vaccine. Great. That warms the cockles and muscles of my tired old heart.

Naturally, neither the manufacturer nor the GP practice has bothered to point out that the cost to the NHS of each vaccine jab is at least £55 (no doubt shared between the company making the stuff and the doctors who give it).

And the side effects that the GP didn't bother to mention?

Well, the common ones include headache, pain, swelling at the area of the vaccination, itching, bruising, joint pain, muscle pain, fever and rash.

Slightly less common side effects include nausea and swollen glands.

Less common side effects include developing chickenpox, developing shingles, sight problems and, of course, having an anaphylactic shock reaction causing difficulty in breathing or swallowing and with death being a possible consequence. That's the sort of death that ends up with a coffin and a spot in the local cemetery.

And what exactly does this doubtless profitable-for-all-concerned-vaccine contain?

Well, my GP didn't bother to tell me that either but I can reveal that he (or she) wants to inject me with a delightful mixture of the live varicella-zoster virus (the live virus you will note) to which has been added sucrose, gelatin, sodium chloride, potassium chloride, disodium phosphate, sodium hydroxide, urea and some other doubtless really good stuff.

I decided to pass on the invitation, thank you very much.

I thought I'd be safer to take my chances with shingles.


## SIGHT

Having your eyes tested is one of only two regular check-ups worth having from a professional. (The other is going to the dentist to have your teeth and gums examined.)

Most people who are over 65 will already need reading glasses since the need usually arises at the age of 45 to 55. Reading vision rarely deteriorates with greater age, so the reading glasses that suited you at 60 should suffice for quite a few years. By and large, if you can see to read reasonably well don't be tricked into spending big money on buying new spectacles every couple of years unless you really want a pair with bright yellow flyaway frames.

A decent optician will also check for glaucoma, cataracts and macular degeneration.

I suggest that you go to a decent optician rather than one in a chain. I once visited a branch of a well-known chain of opticians and was told (quite incorrectly) that I had macular degeneration and should take some (expensive) medication that they could sell me. I subsequently found that I did not have macular degeneration at all and did not need the expensive medication I had been sold.

On another occasion, at another optician, I had my eyes tested by a teenager (he looked about 14 but I suppose he could have been a young looking 16-year-old) and found, to my horror, that my visual fields were appallingly restricted. The youth was testing me on one of those screens upon which little lights appear at random. The person being tested is expected to say whenever a light appears. It's a simple but effective and apparently fool proof test. As a doctor, I was worried to find that I had a massive visual field defect. This can suggest a number of disorders, none of them terribly promising. But peering closely at the screen, I realised that it was very dirty. I asked the youth if he minded if I wiped the screen with a handkerchief. He seemed surprised but said he did not mind. When I had cleaned the screen, I asked him to repeat the test. This he did. We then discovered that there was absolutely nothing wrong with my visual fields for I could see all the little lights as they were lit up.

I often wondered how many people had been sent to their doctor, and thence to hospital, because no one at that wretched store had bothered to clean the screen they were using.

It has also been my experience that opticians will often attempt to sell new spectacles to patients when the change in visual acuity is marginal at best.

So, find an optician you can trust and stick with him or her.


## SUPPOSITORY

Suppositories are jelly-like preparations, usually formed in the shape of a small bullet, which are designed to be inserted into the rectum where they will dissolve. Suppositories can be used very safely and effectively to give a prescription drug to a patient. Sadly, many patients suspect that any doctor who prescribes a suppository must be either French (since the French are known to favour drugs prescribed as suppositories rather than as tablets or capsules) or something of a pervert (or, possibly, both). This is a rather sad misconception. Drugs given in suppository form are absorbed very effectively but are obviously unlikely to upset the stomach lining, and the rectal mucosa is far less sensitive to foreign substances. So, if your doctor wants to prescribe a drug in suppository form then I suggest that you accept the prescription gratefully. Drugs given as suppositories have all the advantages of drugs given by mouth but far fewer of the side effects.

# SURGERY

It is generally accepted that at least a quarter of all surgical operations performed are unnecessary. The real figure is much higher – probably half.

For some types of surgery for example: heart surgery, tonsillectomies, circumcisions, caesarian sections for pregnant women and hysterectomies – the percentage of unnecessary operations is almost certainly much, much higher than that.

At least 90% of all heart surgery is unnecessary.

With many operations (such as hernia repair) the downside is often considerably greater than the upside.

Operations are done unnecessarily for a huge variety of reasons.

Some – particularly those performed on private patients – may be done because the surgeon needs the cash because his boat needs repainting.

And some unnecessary operations are done because it's easier to cut open a patient than it is to think about alternatives. If you go to a Ford garage, the salesman will recommend a Ford motor car. If you visit a surgeon he will recommend surgery.

As the years go by, so the number of unnecessary operations continues to increase.

And it isn't just a problem because of the unnecessary pain and discomfort that patients have to put up with.

At least 1% of the patients who undergo surgery will die on the operating table or in the ward afterwards. One in every 100 patients who goes into hospital for an operation does not walk out again afterwards.

Of course, some patients are very ill when they are wheeled into the operating theatre.

And some patients would have died without surgery.

Many of those patients were perfectly healthy when they are taken into the operating theatre. They were having surgery because they had been persuaded by doctors that it was necessary, or that it would in some way improve the quality of their lives.

Back in 1988 (in a book called *The Health Scandal*) I reported that coronary artery bypass surgery (the commonest procedure performed in cardiac surgery) had been in use for nearly 30 years without anyone trying to find out how patients' everyday lives were affected by the operation.

When a survey was eventually done, it was found that whereas nearly half of the patients who had the operation had been working right up to the time of surgery, three months after the operation, only just over a third of the men were working. And a year after the operation, nearly half of the patients were still not working. In other words, the operation had little positive effect on patients' lives but did put a good many out of action for some time. And there were, of course, a number of patients who died as a result of surgical complications.

A bypass operation takes several hours to perform, consumes a good deal of hospital time and professional skill and can be a physically and mentally exhausting experience for a patient and his family. There is a one in 30 risk that a patient undergoing coronary artery bypass surgery will be dead within 30 days of the operation. The mortality rate varies from surgeon to surgeon but it can be as high as 20% and anything up to a quarter of patients having the operation have heart attacks either while on the operating table or shortly afterwards.

And what makes the medical profession's enthusiasm for coronary artery surgery even more bizarre is the fact that patients who have symptoms of heart disease don't need surgery at all, but stand a better chance of recovering if they are put on a regime which includes a vegan diet, gentle exercise and relaxation. (I described the utterly convincing evidence for this in my book *How To Stop Your Doctor Killing You*, which was first published in 1996. The chapter is entitled *Conquer Heart Disease Without Pills Or Surgery*.)

I can understand cardiac surgeons promoting heart surgery – it is for them a major source of income – but what the hell are GPs doing still referring so many patients for heart surgery?

Any GP who does so should be struck off the medical register and have his stethoscope stuffed up a suitably ill-designed orifice.


## SUSCEPTIBILITY

The elderly are more susceptible to illness (particularly infection) than the young. And so if you walk into a shop and someone is sneezing and coughing without covering their mouth, you should walk out and go somewhere else.

An infection that it is annoying to a 20-year-old could kill an 80-year-old.

# T

## TELEPHONE

Do not answer the telephone if you do not know who is calling or
are not expecting a call. Most telephone companies now provide a
service which tells you the identity of the person calling. These
enable you to avoid time-wasting calls from salesmen, politician and
charities.

## THUGS

Many young thugs and criminals target older people because they
are seen as vulnerable and easy prey. Unbelievable as it might be,
our world is now overpopulated with individuals who have plumbed
new depths of cowardice and greed.

When you are outside in the world, the safest thing to do is to
avoid dark alleyways and badly lit streets. The evil, little bastards
who like hitting old ladies and old gentlemen on the head, prefer to
skulk in dark corners. Since most streets are badly lit these days, that
means not going out in the dark. So be it.

There are things you can do to protect yourself in your own home.
First, never open your door to anyone you aren't expecting or who
doesn't have an appointment – this includes people masquerading as
meter readers or television license investigators or anyone from the
council's recycling gestapo who has come to tell you that you are
going to be punished because your yoghurt cartons haven't been
properly ironed. The chances of you opening your door to a stranger
and benefiting from the experience are very low indeed.

Have a good chain and lock fitted to your door.

If you have a dog, consider buying a large, bad-tempered one
with fangs. Have a peephole fitted to your door so that you can see
who is there. Better still, have a Judas hole which consists of a small
opening rather than just a little glass peephole. If a caller turns up

with a bundle of ten pound notes they want to give you then they can pop them through the Judas and then bugger off.

Remember that anyone who knocks on your door to tell you that your driveway needs repairing or your roof needs attention will be a conman. Keep a garden implement at hand (a hoe or fork or spade will do nicely) and if you do open the door and they put their foot in it then threaten to use your garden tool to persuade them to remove their impediment.

Do not be gentle but shout an apology as they hobble off down your garden path.

# TRANQUILLISERS

In nearly 50 years, I have written more about benzodiazepines and other tranquillisers, sleeping tablets and sedatives than anyone in the world. And I have done three books on drug addiction.

A fat lot of good it all did.

The tranquilliser problem today is as bad as it was back in1973 when I first started campaigning.

Today, most cases of alleged dementia are a result of old people being drugged by bad doctors.

For decades, I have watched the medical industry suppress and repel the truth.

No medical organisations are on the side of the patient. The British Medical Association (BMA), for example is a trade union with strong drug company links. The union receives millions from the drug industry (in payment for advertisements placed in publications such as the *British Medical Journal*) and they will never be on the side of the patient.

For years, BMA spokesmen actively opposed my concerns about benzodiazepines. There is no little irony in the fact that the British Medical Association now appears to be taking part in attempts to deal with tranquilliser addiction. It would be more helpful if the BMA were to criticise its own members who ignored prescribing advice and created the problem that exists.

The Department of Health, mortally influenced by the drug industry and a bought and paid for medical establishment, spends gazillions on the relatively few people who have chosen to take mildly addictive drugs such as cocaine and heroin (not sold by the drug industry) but nothing on the millions who have through no fault of their own been damaged by benzodiazepines (sold by the drug industry).

It isn't difficult to see a pattern there.

Back in 1988, the Government (admitting it was responding to my first 15 years of campaigning) warned doctors that the benzodiazepines should not be prescribed for more than two to four weeks.

Doctors have taken absolutely no bloody notice of this guidance.

Originally introduced specifically to help calm extremely nervous and agitated patients (and for use as anaesthetics) benzodiazepines were, by the time they reached their peak, being prescribed for just about every illness known to man or woman. I've met people for whom they had been prescribed as treatments for backache, menopausal problems, pre-menstrual tension, migraine, high blood pressure, alopecia and urinary tract infections. It got to the point where doctors were handing out prescriptions for benzodiazepine tranquillisers whenever they didn't know what else to do. There was never any evidence to show that drugs were effective in treating all these different conditions.

Benzodiazepine addiction has for decades been the world's biggest drug addiction problem.

Countless millions of prescriptions a year are still being written for benzodiazepine tranquillisers. Over a third of the prescriptions are for more than eight weeks supply.

What a bloody profession.

Any doctor who signs a prescription for a benzodiazepine (such as Valium) for more than two weeks is not fit to practise medicine and would, if the General Medical Council did what it is supposed to do, be struck off the medical register.

I now think that, instead of relying on the good sense and integrity of doctors, the majority of patients should take control of their own destiny by refusing to take tranquillisers, sedatives or sleeping tablets for more than two weeks. Better still, refuse to take them at all.

# TRAVEL

If you are travelling by train or aeroplane, don not be afraid to tell the company in advance that you are old and/or disabled and will need help. If you think that there will be too much walking at the other end, insist on being met by a person with a wheelchair and play merry hell if it isn't there. Demand attention. If you don't receive the help you need then have a noisy hissy fit. Complain, complain and complain again. Be ruthless and remorseless. Ask if they would treat a VIP this way. Demand to know the name and address of the chairman of the company. Keep telephone numbers for a few newspapers and TV or radio stations in your own phone and let it be known that you will be reporting the incident.

If all else fails, a collapse on the airport or station floor should bring useful attention.

Remember to say thank you afterwards.

# TRAVEL FOR TREATMENT

For as long as it continues to exist, the NHS will continue to decline. Moreover, private care (currently providing the sort of level of service provided by the NHS two or three decades ago) will also deteriorate. Many consultants who were previously working exclusively in the NHS have carried their bad manners into private practice and many patients don't know enough to expect better. Even private hospitals have deteriorated, because of the appalling standard set by the NHS. Visit a private hospital and the chances are that you will sit in a crowded waiting room. After a lengthy wait, you will be hurried in to see your consultant who will rush through your consultation so that she (or he) can get onto the next patient. 'Payment in advance please, please see the receptionist. Cash, cheques and all major credit cards taken.' Private patients now routinely have to wait days (or weeks) to receive the results of simple blood tests, X-ray tests or tissue sample tests. And they have to wait weeks (or months) for essential, life-saving surgery. Paying privately in Britain now buys you better food, slightly more polite nurses and a television set all of your own that you don't have to feed with tokens. But it doesn't buy you better medical care (which is, I suspect, what most people suspect they're going to get when they spend vast amounts of money on private health insurance) though it does, importantly, buy you a good chance of avoiding a deadly antibiotic-resistant infection.

Normal health care practice in other countries is to receive test results within an hour or so and, if you have a serious disorder needing treatment, to receive that treatment within a few days. Not even private patients get that level of care in Britain today.

So, not surprisingly, a growing number of Britons now go abroad for health care; travelling to India or Thailand for medical and surgical treatment. Hospitals in these countries are far cleaner, far more modern and far better equipped than British hospitals. Patients go to hospitals and clinics in Poland, Bulgaria and Japan. And they go not just because they can avoid long waiting lists or because private hospital care is much cheaper than it is in the UK but because they know that they will be treated better and they will be safer. There is far less risk of infection in most other countries. Patients go abroad for major operations and they go for the treatment of relatively minor ailments; many even go abroad for dental treatment.

And the prices (which often include first class hotel accommodation for accompanying relatives) are, even when the costs of travel are included, often considerably lower than the price of treatment in the UK.

For example, a cataract removal in the UK will cost you the best part of £3,000. The same operation would cost around £500 in Bulgaria. A coronary bypass would cost £ 15,000 in the UK and £5,000. A hip replacement would cost £10,000 in the UK and £3,000 in Tunisia. A full set of dentures which would cost £700 in the UK would cost £200 in Latvia.

The private surgery prices in the UK are high because NHS waiting lists are deliberately manipulated, and cruelly long, and private hospitals and doctors take advantage of the demand by pushing their prices sky high.

Patients travel abroad not just because operations and treatments are cheaper outside the UK (and do not involve a long waiting time) but also because they know that the medical and nursing care will be far superior, that they will receive better food and that their relatives will be better received. How embarrassing it is to have to write that. Some hospitals in the Far East have turned non-emergency, elective surgery into a quasi-holiday experience.

The quality of medical care in Britain will continue to deteriorate because the NHS's answer to all the bad things that happen is not to train people better (or, heaven forbid, to punish the worst offenders) but to add another layer of impenetrable bureaucracy, separating the people with the power from the people making the decisions, and to ensure that no one can ever be held responsible for anything they do.

The people with the power protect the lowly people who take the decisions because that helps to protect the position of the people with the power. It's an unwritten rule. No one must be punished or even reprimanded because once you start down that slippery slope you end up with some higher level official having to accept responsibility and that cannot be contemplated. And so nothing ever improves. Problems merely create more cover ups. The only concern is to avoid anyone having to say 'sorry', or admit that they have made a mistake.

Patients and their relatives may remain unsatisfied, aggrieved or concerned that someone else will suffer in exactly the same way that they did. But none of this seems to matter as long as no jobs are lost or even threatened. Hospital bureaucrats prefer to pay off a litigant (without admitting liability or having to resign) than to defend a case in court.

It is a telling fact that Britain's NHS now spends more on lawyers than on doctors.


## TRICKSTERS

There is nothing you can buy (no medicines and no health foods) which will slow the ageing process or increase longevity.

Anyone who tries to sell you something with such a purpose is a confidence trickster. Kick them on the ankles.

# U

## UNCARING

My wife and I recently stood on the platform at the Gare du Nord in Paris and stared, in horror, as Eurostar staff watched two elderly travellers struggling to lift their suitcases onto the train and into their first class carriage. The Eurostar staff just stood there and did nothing. In recent years, there has been a notable deterioration in the quality of service offered everywhere. Just a few years ago, the Eurostar staff would always help. These days they never do. This sort of uncaring behaviour is now pretty standard at railway stations. (My wife and I helped the struggling couple but we were fighting to lift our own cases up the steep steps and onto the train.)

## UTILITIES

The biggest confidence tricksters are not the ones offering to put an eighth of an inch of tarmacadam down on your drive but the people who are selling you electricity, gas and insurance. It is no accident that your utility bills are incomprehensible – that's the way they are designed.

Utility companies and insurance companies doubtless now have special obfuscation departments which exist solely to make bills and communications impossible to understand.

Insurance companies, like phone companies, banks and utilities, punish loyal and regular customers – this affects the older citizens more than most because they tend to be loyal.

Sadly, the only solution, the only way to fight these greedy, merciless, disloyal, murdering bastards, is to look around every 12 months and switch your supplier.

If you don't do this then your utility company will put you onto their 'standard' traffic and your bills will be two, three or even four times as high as they should be.

# V

## VACCINATIONS

Once you pass into your 60s, you will suddenly find yourself enormously popular with your doctor. He or she won't want to visit you at home, of course. If you want to be ill, you will probably have to make an appointment for three weeks ahead and then make do with a wet-behind-the-ears junior trainee or the practice nurse. The GP with whom you are registered will be far too busy counting his money to see you.

But you will receive regular letters inviting you to visit the surgery to be vaccinated. Sometimes it will be the flu vaccine. Sometimes it will be something else. But the chances are that once you reach a certain age then the vaccination offers will come pretty thick and fast.

Do not however assume that this is a consequence of any genuine concern for your wellbeing. Your doctor wants to vaccinate you (or, more accurately, to tell his practice nurse to vaccinate you) because he is paid vast amounts of money to vaccinate everyone.

Doctors have been bought lock, stock and syringe barrel.

Drug companies make huge amounts of money out of selling vaccines. And the establishment has fiddled the evidence, and denied or suppressed the inconvenient truths, in order to promote the official point of view. In Britain, I have been banned from speaking to doctors on this subject. Debates about vaccination are unknown.

Those who promote vaccines often claim that vaccination programmes have reduced illness, prevented millions of deaths and are the main reason why the average life expectation has risen.

These are all barefaced lies.

The whole vaccination story is one of the great modern scandals of our time. The entire medical profession (at least the part of it in general practice) has been bribed by the drug industry, working through the Government and using taxpayers' money.

Most doctors, whether working as hospital consultants, GPs or public health officials, know very little about vaccination. The majority simply follow the establishment line, never question what they are told by the drug industry and dismiss all critics of vaccination as dangerous lunatics.

And doctors know nothing about the dangers of the damned vaccines they so happily jab into patients' arms. Question the whole damned sordid business and these ill-educated propagandists (who know nothing about the risks of the toxic mixtures they are promoting) will throw up their hands in horror. Ask them for some evidence that vaccines are safe and effective and they become hysterical.

If a doctor wants to vaccinate you then insist that he confirms in writing that the vaccine is both entirely safe and absolutely essential. You may notice his enthusiasm for the vaccine suddenly diminish.

# W

## WEATHER

The weather kills a lot of elderly people.

In the winter, people die of the cold. In the summer they die of the heat.

If you go out in cold weather, make sure that you are well protected from the elements. Carry an umbrella (which can also be used as a stabilising walking stick) and wear shoes with good, grippy soles. Stay inside if the weather is particularly bad. Supermarkets will deliver food these days and corner shops always have done so. Don't be like William Harrison, who was President of the US for a month and died of pneumonia because he insisted on delivering a three hour inaugural speech in the pouring rain.

If the weather is hot, stay out of the sun and the hottest rooms in your home. Drink plenty of fluids to replace what your body is losing and cool your body down by putting a wet something next to your skin.

## WORRIED LOOK

Doctors often look worried. This isn't necessarily anything to worry about. It may mean that the doctor doesn't know your name. Try introducing your own name, age and address into the conversation as subtly as possible. You should soon see a look of relief replacing the worried look.

## WORLD WIDE WEB

Be sceptical about everything you see or read on the internet. The computer was the world's worst invention. The internet was the second worst invention.

The internet can undoubtedly be useful. If you use a grocery website you can have your anchovies, caviar and gentleman's relish all brought down to your door by a bloke (or blokess) in a van.

And you can use the internet to send your utility company your correct meter readings. This will stop them using an estimated bill to gouge extra money out of your account. (Estimated utility bills are always far higher than your real-life bills could possibly be.)

But the damned thing has got completely out of hand in recent years and today every company on the planet has got into the comfortable habit of using the internet as an excuse to enable it to cut costs.

If you try to telephone anyone these days, the chances are that you will, when you have tippy toed your way through a maze of instructions and chosen from an always useless list of options, be met with a voice telling that because of 'exceptionally high call volumes' their agents/consultants are all very busy.

You will be assured that 'your call is very important to us' and that your call will be taken 'as soon as one of our agents/consultants becomes available'.

This is all balderdash of course.

The phrase 'we are experiencing exceptionally high call volumes' is the first thing they record and they play it all day long. If you ring at 3 a.m. on a Wednesday, they'll be 'experiencing exceptionally high call volumes'.

All companies which use telephones have fired most of their staff and their customer service department consists of a couple of over-worked and under-paid slaves working in a dirty office somewhere in Asia.

While you wait for someone to become available, you will be bombarded with constant messages (designed to ensure that you can't do anything useful while you wait for your call to be dealt with) and exhortations to use their website.

And that's the nub of the thing. They don't want you to speak to a real person. Even when they live in Asia and get paid pitiful wages, agents and consultants are expensive because the poor sods will insist on being paid. If you don't throw them a handful of beads every now and again you can bet your ass that some interfering human rights organisation will expose you and claim that you've been exploiting the little buggers.

All big companies (and a lot of small ones) want you to use their website. If you persist with the telephone they'll punish you by making you wait half an hour or an hour. They know that you'll eventually give up. And when you've been through this agony three or four times you'll see sense and use the bloody website.

# X

There is no 'X' worth including. Why put one in just for the sake of it? This is an honest book.

# Y

## YOUR BODY

Here are some truths you should know about the older body:

The older body recovers more slowly.

The older body is less effective at protecting itself.

The older body heals rather less effectively.

The older body is more vulnerable.

The older body is more susceptible to illness and likely to suffer more.

# Z

See 'X'.

# APPENDIX

Coleman's Laws
Here are my 12 laws – designed to help you survive medical care.

*Coleman's 1st Law of Medicine*
If you are receiving treatment for an existing disease and you develop new symptoms then, until proved otherwise, you should assume that the new symptoms are caused by the treatment you are receiving.

*Coleman's 2nd Law of Medicine*
There is no point in having tests done unless the results will affect your treatment.

*Coleman's 3rd Law of Medicine*
If the treatment doesn't work then you should consider the possibility that the diagnosis might be wrong. This is particularly true when several treatments have been tried.

*Coleman's 4th Law of Medicine*
Screening examinations and check-ups are more profitable for doctors than for patients.

*Coleman's 5th Law of Medicine*
It is doctors, not patients, who need annual check-ups.

*Coleman's 6th Law of Medicine*
Hospitals are not suitable places for sick people. If you must go into one, you should get out as quickly as you can.

*Coleman's 7th Law of Medicine*
There are fashions in medicine just as much as there are fashions in clothes. The difference is that whereas badly conceived fashions in clothes are only likely to embarrass you, ill-conceived fashions in

medicine may kill you. The fashions in medicine have, by and large, as much scientific validity as the fashions in the rag trade.

*Coleman's 8th Law of Medicine*
The medical establishment will always take decisions on health matters which benefit industry, Government and the medical profession, rather than patients. And the Government will always take decisions on health matters which benefit the State rather than individual patients. What you read or hear about medicine and health matters will have more to do with the requirements of the pharmaceutical industry and the Government, than the genuine needs of patients.

*Coleman's 9th Law of Medicine*
Doctors and nurses know little or nothing about staying healthy. In particular, doctors and nurses know nothing useful about food, diet and healthy eating. (Sadly, the same is true of nutritionists and dieticians).

*Coleman's 10th Law of Medicine*
There are no holistic healers. There are only holistic patients.

*Coleman's 11th Law of Medicine*
There is no such thing as minor surgery.

*Coleman's 12th Law of Medicine*
Some patients will always be treated more equally than others.

Taken from *Coleman's Laws* by Vernon Coleman

Made in the USA
Middletown, DE
02 May 2023

29896046R00092